MONTGOMERY COLLEGE LIBRARY
ROCKVILLE CAMPUS

D. H.
LAWRENCE
& SUSAN HIS COW

D. H. LAWRENCE
& *SUSAN HIS COW*

WILLIAM YORK TINDALL

COLUMBIA UNIVERSITY

NEW YORK

COOPER SQUARE PUBLISHERS, INC.

1972

Originally Published 1939
Copyright 1939 by Columbia University Press
Reprinted by Permission of Columbia University Press
Published 1972 by Cooper Square Publishers, Inc.
59 Fourth Avenue, New York, N. Y. 10003
International Standard Book Number 0-8154-0436-0
Library of Congress Card Catalog Number 72-85664

Printed in the United States of America

TO CECILIA

PREFACE

IN his back yard at Taos, D. H. Lawrence had a cow
named Susan. This creature, whose temper seems to
have deserved neither respect nor love, claimed the respect and love of her master. He celebrated her in one of
his essays, ". . . . Love Was Once a Little Boy," mentioned her frequently in others, and allowed himself to
be photographed with her, as the reader of the collected
letters may see for himself. To Lawrence, Susan was a
cow, good to pursue with loud cries and good to milk in
the cool of the evening:

> Cow Susan by the forest's rim
> A black-eyed Susan was to him
> And nothing more—

But, though he denies it in these playful verses, she was
something more. To him she was also a religious object
and a symbol of life and salvation. "How can I equi-
librate myself with my black cow Susan?" he asked.
". . . There *is* a sort of relation between us. And this
relation is part of the mystery of love. . . . The queer
cowy mystery of her is her changeless cowy desirableness." [1]

Some may be inclined to put Lawrence down for a
fool; for it cannot be denied that he sounds foolish. But
one must remember that Lawrence was a man of great
gifts, probably a man of what we call genius, that a

[1] *Reflections on the Death of a Porcupine,* pp. 164–76.

genius is not always reasonable, and that, when understood, he may seem less foolish than at first. The critic's
first duty to a genius is to try to understand his meaning.

The questions before the critic of Lawrence are these:
Why should a man of great gifts have tried to know a
cow, even a symbolical cow? Why should he have approached her, beneath a superficial levity, with a kind of
religious awe, with feelings more appropriate to High
Mass? And why should an adoring company of readers
assist so solemnly at his services?

I have found in Susan not only a problem requiring
solution but a symbol in which Lawrence's life and work
are conveniently expressed, and I have used her as a
point of departure. Starting with the problem of Susan
and going back to what led up to it, we may arrive at an
answer to our questions and at an understanding of
much in Lawrence's work—of that part which seems most
foolish and of that to which merit may not be denied.
I am afraid that, in spite of the title of this book, which
may have led to other expectations, I shall deal less with
Susan than with the road to Susan. In following this road
and its several byways, I shall consider Lawrence's troubles, his efforts to find relief, the development of what
he called his philosophy, and the effect of his philosophy
upon his art.

I have also taken Susan as a symbol of wider significance, as a symbol by which the plight and the aspirations of many artists of our day may be expressed. If we
understand Lawrence and Susan, we may come to a
better understanding of some of the problems of our
literature, society, judgment, and taste. To Lawrence,

Susan was a way of salvation. To us she may be a way of understanding; for many of the most distinguished men of letters of the last fifty years have had their Susans. I propose, by following the road to Lawrence's cow, to encounter her sister cows and to approach a general problem of our times.

My search for the meaning of Susan has led me through Lawrence's prose,[2] which the publication of *Phoenix* and of the various collections of letters has made at last substantially available. I have also looked into the memorial volumes issued by almost all who enjoyed Lawrence's acquaintance. To these writers of memoirs, especially to the Brewsters, Frederick Carter, E. T., Catherine Carswell, Mabel Dodge Luhan, Knud Merrild, and Mrs. Lawrence, I am indebted. The growing body of primary material of this kind which has appeared since his death has given us more information about Lawrence than about any of his contemporaries and has made him both a suitable subject for further investigation and a splendid center from which to set out on a study of his times.

For this reason it is odd that so little attention has been paid to Lawrence by scholars and historians. The few scholarly essays which have been devoted to Lawrence, such as the recent books by Ernest Seillière and Paul de Reul, have not been scholarly enough to uncover what had been unknown or to be immune from the prepossessions of the authors. But we have had acute psychological studies, like that of J. Middleton Murry,

[2] And through the verse as well; but since the evidence in the verse is meager and no more than parallel to that in the prose, I have confined my remarks to the prose, citing the poetical evidence in the notes.

and many excellent personal and critical reactions to
Lawrence, like those by Richard Aldington, Aldous
Huxley, F. R. Leavis, Horace Gregory, Hugh Kingsmill,
and Wyndham Lewis. Such essays not infrequently take
the form of notes on the state of the critic's soul in the
presence of genius.

This essay is neither the story of a critic's soul nor the
statement of an enthusiasm. It is an effort to account for
Lawrence historically, to place him in the intellectual,
social, and literary movements of his time, to show how
his response to his personal problems took its character
from what was going on around him. Putting a prophet
into a pigeonhole may strike the enthusiast as improper
or useless, but if it adds, as it should, to the understanding of Lawrence's work and of our times, it is neither.
Moreover, enthusiasm, like censure, is properly, though
not generally, directed at what is understood.

The conclusions of this essay are based in part upon
the discovery of facts without which Lawrence's meaning
must remain unclear and his reader's enthusiasm mis-
directed. Lawrence's interest in theosophy and yoga,
for example, had escaped attention, and the occult and
anthropological sources of *The Plumed Serpent, Apocalypse,* and several other pieces had not been traced. Acquaintance with these matters may give occasion to
some, perhaps, for fresh enthusiasm, but it is more likely
to impair for others the value of a writer who depends so
much upon message. I am not, however, unwilling to
take this risk.

These new facts were uncovered largely by an ex-
amination of Lawrence's reading. An approach of this

sort to a writer with a message is almost always profitable
and likely to make the origin and nature of the message
plain, but this approach to Lawrence is difficult. The
evidence for his reading is obscured by oblique or partial
reference in his letters and essays or by his silence.
Lawrence rarely recalled the names of authors. He was
careless about titles and sometimes confused one with
another. His opinions about books as about places varied
with his moods. The occasional fault of all but angels,
perhaps, became habitual with him: he generally condemned what he found most useful. Had he been a more
temperate man, his opinions about his reading might
have been as important for our purposes as his reading.
But with Lawrence we must be contented with noting
his use rather than his abuse of books, and we must remember that he cannot be blamed for his nature or for
failing to aid a search which he could have neither anticipated nor welcomed. With some pains, however, I
have been able to discover from his writings many of
the books he read, together with the use he made of
them, and I have been able to supplement these findings
by correspondence with his friends. Mrs. Lawrence, who
read the books her husband read, endured my tiresome
questions and was very helpful. Mrs. Mabel Dodge
Luhan, Mrs. Julian Huxley, Lady Ottoline Morrell, and
Mr. Witter Bynner kindly told me what they knew.
With this aid and by this method I have been able to
follow the road to the symbolical Susan.

The first steps along this road were taken in the sum-
mer of 1936. My attention had been directed to Lawrence by my encounter with several members of what

must be called his cult, by my sudden recognition of the resemblance between Lawrence and Bunyan, whom I had been studying, and by my discovery of Susan while preparing a lecture on contemporary literature. I was not unaware that Sir Walter Raleigh had said: "Whosoever in writing a modern Historie shall follow truth too neare the heeles, it may haply strike out his teeth." And I knew the peril to be greater in following too near the heels of a cow. Perhaps I had the courage to proceed along my road because I did not know at that time that a reviewer in *The Times Literary Supplement* was to chide a French critic for being dispassionate about Lawrence, for failing to be "intensely excited" by one who was "assuredly the most powerful genius in contemporary English literature." [3] Perhaps I had the courage to proceed dispassionately to certain unfavorable conclusions because at that time I had not heard Archibald MacLeish read a threatening poem directed against the detractors of D. H. Lawrence. But ignorance gave boldness to my preliminary steps, and I proceeded from the American Museum of Natural History, where my studies appropriately commenced, to Richmond, Virginia, where in December, 1936, I made a report on my findings before the Modern Language Association. Later I embodied the principal conclusions of what are now Chapters IV and V of this study in an article published in the *Sewanee Review* (April–June, 1937), from which I am now reprinting certain sections with the kind permission of the editor.

[3] Review of Paul de Reul's *L'Œuvre de D. H. Lawrence,* January 8, 1938. Cf. the issue of June 18, 1938.

For permission to quote material from Lawrence's *Fantasia of the Unconscious, Phoenix, Women in Love, Psychoanalysis and the Unconscious, Apocalypse, Sea and Sardinia, Kangaroo, Aaron's Rod, Last Poems,* and *Studies in Classic American Literature* and from *The Letters of D. H. Lawrence* I am extremely indebted to the Viking Press, Inc., which controls the American rights to these volumes. Passages from Lawrence's *Plumed Serpent, Mornings in Mexico, St. Mawr, Lady Chatterley's Lover,* "Glad Ghosts," and "Sun" are reprinted by permission of and special arrangement with Alfred A. Knopf, Inc., authorized publishers for America. I am very grateful to the Centaur Press of Philadelphia for permission to quote from Lawrence's *Reflections on the Death of a Porcupine.* By arrangement with the representatives of Mrs. Lawrence and William Heinemann, Ltd., who control the British rights to the abovementioned works, I have also been permitted to make certain quotations. By the kind permission of the Clarendon Press, Oxford, I have reprinted a passage from Lawrence's *Movements in European History.* I am greatly obliged to Harcourt, Brace and Company, Inc., for permitting me to use selections from Catherine Carswell's *Savage Pilgrimage* and from I. A. Richard's *Principles of Literary Criticism;* to the Macmillan Company for permission to quote from W. B. Yeats's *Autobiographies* and *Essays;* to Jonathan Cape, Ltd., for a passage from Samuel Butler's *Life and Habit;* to Charles Scribner's Sons for a passage from Thomas Wolfe's *Story of a Novel;* to Martin Secker & Warburg, Ltd., for passages from *Early Life of D. H. Lawrence* by Ada Lawrence and G.

Stuart Gelder and from *D. H. Lawrence, Reminiscences and Correspondence,* by Earl and Achsah Brewster.

I wish to express my gratitude to Mrs. Lawrence and to Dr. George Vaillant for giving me hitherto unpublished material about Lawrence. My thanks are also due to Dr. Lincoln Reis for information about art and prudence and to Professor O. J. Campbell for a most valuable suggestion and much encouragement. By his criticism Professor Ernest Hunter Wright has increased the debt I owe him for many favors. As my mother read the proofs she offered invaluable comments on natural history. I could not have managed without Cecilia, my wife, who indulged my monologues and patiently admired the freshly written paragraph before correcting it.

W. Y. T.

Columbia University
June 22, 1939

CONTENTS

D. H.
LAWRENCE
& SUSAN HIS COW

'Tis all in peeces, all cohaerence gone:
All just supply, and all Relation:
Prince, Subject, Father, Sonne, are things forgot,
For every man alone thinkes he hath got
To be a Phoenix, and that then can bee
None of that kinde, of which he is, but hee.
This is the worlds condition now . . .

—John Donne, *An Anatomie of the World*

CHAPTER ONE

A PILLAR OF SALT BY DAY

LAWRENCE'S pursuit of Susan and the religious character of this pastoral distraction can be understood
only in the light of his nature, the circumstances of his
life, and his spiritual temper. When these matters have
been made clear, what went on in his back yard at Taos
may be regarded with disapproval but no longer with
surprise. Indeed, we can wonder only that his efforts to
find relief from a painful fortune drove him to no worse
than the pasture. Lawrence was doomed by his nature
and by circumstance to a strange excess and to a useless
struggle, of which his books and the affair of Susan are
the memorials.

He was born and bred in a blighted mining town near
Nottingham, among the broken bedsprings and rusty
canisters of Mr. Eliot's hell and of Mr. Joyce's fever
dream. This detestable place was made more detestable
by the contrast of haystacks, flowers, and cows on the surviving farms in the vicinity. To have been bred among
the properties of the Waste Land might be accounted a
privilege by an Eliot, who could face them and raise them
to the first intensity as images in a poem, but Lawrence,
who did not feel the fascination of the horrible, wanted
to go away from there. The setting was more congenial
to his father, a Methodist coal miner. Lawrence the son
preferred superior persons.

His mother was a superior person whose aspirations

toward gentility and whose sobriety were stimulated by the intemperance of her husband. The children of this unfortunate marriage, especially Lawrence the favorite son, sided with their mother. As devoted to him as he to her, she saved her favorite from the mines but not from herself. That he suffered from the complaint of Oedipus at least until maturity and perhaps throughout his life has been affirmed—and there is no reason to doubt it— in the memoirs by E. T., Frieda Lawrence, and J. Middleton Murry. His relationship with E. T., his first love, who chooses to conceal her name under these initials, was impaired by this classical fixation, as her book and as *Sons and Lovers* explain at some length; and Frieda Lawrence, his wife, tells of the annoyance it caused her during her flight with Lawrence to the Continent. Both he and those around him were aware of his trouble long before they knew of Freud.

This impediment to a normal life, which added another discomfort to those of place and class, seems to have been only one among others. It is likely from the conduct of Lawrence's heroes in *The White Peacock, Aaron's Rod, Kangaroo,* and *Women in Love,* as it is from the affair of the farmer in Cornwall and from that of Clarence in Taos (if Mrs. Luhan is accurate in reporting these episodes), that Lawrence had more than the proper regard for his fellow man. For this reason, his experience with women was a disappointment to him.

His body was equally disappointing: thin, frail, sickly, and far from handsome, it seemed not to have been designed for love. The sniffles and the meager chest from which he suffered as a boy led to pneumonia and then to tuberculosis. This distemper may have warmed his sensuous imagination as it decreased his flesh, but though its effects were apparent, they struck some observers less than his imperfect features. Many who were diverted by his soul could ignore the flesh or see beneath it. David Garnett, however, speaks of Lawrence's underbred and mongrel appearance; and after her disappointment with his soul, Mrs. Luhan was able to contemplate his vulgar nose, to which she attributes more importance than it deserves. This ailing man of no appearance grew a beard which, however suggestive of power, covered neither nose nor chest.[1]

The nerves of the bearded lover were naked. Ordinary troubles were more than ordinarily trying to him. He had the sensitivity of a cat, the sensibility of a not too sensible woman,[2] the impatience of Donald Duck. Recoiling from place, experience, and body, he trailed the pageant of his naked nerves through Europe, Asia, Polynesia, and America. From sanatorium and home the envy of sedentary neurotics followed his progress, proving it a literary sensation but making it no more comfortable.

His private and social deficiencies were bad enough, but they were complicated by other vexations and disappointments and by the war. The war was more than tiresome to Lawrence. His soul could not flower, he felt,

[1] Lawrence's sensitivity about his body and his beard is shown in *Kangaroo*, pp. 241, 248, 286. The beard symbolizes his "isolate manhood."

[2] *Kangaroo*, pp. 326–27: he feels that he-men despise him as a "shifty she-man." Knud Merrild in *A Poet and Two Painters* concluded, however, apparently on the grounds that Lawrence made no advances during their winter together, that Lawrence was more manly than he was reputed to be (pp. 103–4, 208).

amid so much iron, his sensitive body shrank from the analytical gaze of inspectors for the draft, and he felt thwarted and caged by the refusal of the government to permit his departure from England. The spies who suspected him of aiding the Germans gave him and his German bride no peace. These troubles, which he was less fitted than most to suffer, were made insufferable by poverty, hostility, and neglect. The banning of *The Rainbow*, a work of the highest moral elevation, for vicious immorality filled the baffled moralist with rage and despair. His hopes of a sympathetic audience and of financial reward for his novels and essays were disappointed, and he had scarcely enough money for food. His efforts to interest George Moore and Arnold Bennett in his work were deficient in knowledge of human nature and in success. Efforts on the part of his friends to get him governmental aid were of no avail. It looked as if he might have to get a job. He felt that society and circumstance had conspired against him, that every hand was lifted against him, that man had made of him an enemy of man. His nerves gave way: "I am almost a lunatic," he exclaimed, and he prayed for the destruction of the world.[3]

Some of his difficulties were the result of his nervousness and some a cause, but the state of the world was independent of him and no less oppressive. He would

[3] *The Letters of D. H. Lawrence*, p. 228. Cf. the poem "The Revolutionary" (*Collected Poems*, II, 136), in which Lawrence imagines he is Samson pulling down the corrupt world upon himself. Knud Merrild's friend Götzsche, after traveling through Mexico with Lawrence, concluded that Lawrence was "a queer snail," who seemed at times to be "absolutely nuts." *A Poet and Two Painters*, pp. 343, 348, 350, 356–57. Cf. *Kangaroo*, pp. 280, 287.

have been unhappy at any time and in any society, but
he found the present too much to endure. He found himself in a society from which science, industry, finance,
and their consequences had stolen beauty, religion, and
order. He saw around him a world of confusion, a world
without a central belief from which to get comfort and
support. He saw that his own predicament was part of a
larger confusion.

As to this, he differed little from other sensitive men
in our times. His discontent and his efforts to find a center or to adjust himself were those of his fellows. But his
difficulties were made more terrible than those of most
men of our times by the thinness of his skin and by his
want of discipline. His inner disorder left him unable to
conquer outer disorder. The story of his life is one of
innumerable attempts and failures to adjust himself to
circumstance or rather, more commonly, to adjust circumstance to himself. He made many brave and foolish
efforts to correct his social and physical deficiencies and
to discover or to invent a society in which he could be
contented.

Marriage to Frieda was Lawrence's most practical attempt to find relief for his nervous and social troubles
and to find a center in an alien world. Their first meeting
had been casual. In April, 1912, Professor Ernest Weekley of Nottingham invited the young poet to tea, but
the imprudent professor had neglected to conceal his
wife, Frieda, daughter of Baron von Richthofen and sister of the future ace. Lawrence looked at Mrs. Weekley
and Mrs. Weekley looked at Lawrence. That day they
talked of Freud, but on Lawrence's second visit they

talked no more. Taking advantage of her husband's absence, and sending away her three children, Mrs. Weekley invited Lawrence to stay the night. Rather than indulge her liberal fancy, Lawrence eloped with her. The professor and his three children deplored her conduct, but, as she observed some years later, it was not she but the wind.

That the relief provided by marriage was incomplete is plain from the continued wandering of his fancy, but it was enough to enable him to suffer what would otherwise have been too much for him. His marriage was most useful to him, perhaps, for the social relief it offered. The daughter of the baron gave to the son of the miner that elevation above his class which the gentility of his mother had recommended to him. By the aid of his baronial wife, Lawrence shook the dust of his class from his feet, and, stepping over the materialistic middle classes with disdain, he found himself least uneasy in the society of such other aristocrats as he could discover. His snobbishness expanded in the company of Lady Ottoline Morrell, Lady Cynthia Asquith, and the Honorable Dorothy Brett.

The imperfect happiness he found in love and aristocracy failed to conceal the horror of the world, which gave him "the gruesomes," he said, the more he saw of it.[4] For a time Italy had provided refuge from England, but the war convinced him that Europe was done for and left him without hope except in plans of escape from the City of Destruction. He planned flights to Florida, the Andes, Africa, and the South Seas. In 1915 he said: "I wish I

4 *Letters*, p. 622.

were going to Thibet—or Kamschatka—or Tahiti—to the ultima, ultima, ultima Thule. I feel sometimes I shall go mad, because there is nowhere to go, no 'new world.' " [5] At the end of the war, as soon as he could get a passport, he fled to Italy again, then to Ceylon, to Australia, to New Mexico, then back to Italy. In one of those sudden illuminations which his readers came to expect of him he said: "Whatever flesh I've got on my bones isn't Sitzfleisch . . ." [6]

His wanderings gave him no rest. He never found the place where he could be happy. As soon as he arrived in a new place he wrote enthusiastic letters about it, only to condemn it after a few days or weeks. Jack Grant, the hero of *The Boy in the Bush,* was "always homesick for somewhere else," [7] and the last words of Lawrence's last letter express his inevitable conclusion: "This place no good." [8] His discontent with the here and now shows not so much the nature of the places and times from which he sought escape as his neurotic inability to adjust himself. In his clearer moments Lawrence saw that distant places were "only the negation of what we ourselves stand for and are: and we're rather like Jonahs running from the place we belong." [9] But his clearer moments were few, and he belonged nowhere.

As he fled from place to place, now pursued, now merely accompanied by his nerves, he also tried to find relief through imagination and art. He found that in his novels he could invent a better world, a world in which men somewhat like himself could prosper and expand.

[5] *Ibid.,* p. 226.   [6] *Ibid.,* p. 690.   [7] *The Boy in the Bush,* p. 33.
[8] *Letters,* p. 853.   [9] *Ibid.,* p. 543.

He found delight in presenting the world of ugliness and confusion only to condemn or to destroy it. After the triumph of the good over the actual, pleasures such as he had never known and powers of which he had dreamed could be enjoyed by creatures of his fancy, made outwardly in his image but otherwise his opposite. Daydream and fantasy, which inspire the makers of myths and the industrious psychoanalyst, gave Lawrence what relief he found. His novels and their heroes were at once the symptoms and the cure of his disorder.

The heroes of Lawrence's novels come for the most part from the social class to which he was born and from the mining region. They are small or frail, usually bearded. Each has a gleam in his eye and a way with women and animals. With these advantages his gamekeepers, stableboys, miners, and ambiguous persons arise from their obscurity and discontent to win a lady of importance. These heroes resemble their creator in nature and appearance, and their lives follow the pattern of his own, but they know a fulfillment denied him. Such fantasies, which gave Lawrence a vicarious satisfaction, give his work a tragical significance.

Birkin, the earliest hero of the authentic type, emerged in 1916 when war, marriage, and misery inspired *Women in Love*. The physical frailty of this pedagogue from Nottingham is deceptive, for he is able to overcome Gerald at wrestling if not in love. He possesses Lawrence's contempt of the world and his hopes. By word and example he justifies a life of wandering and restlessness, but he finds adjustment. Lilly, the hero of *Aaron's Rod*, is Birkin under a different name. After him follow Somers, the hero of *Kangaroo;* Jack of *The Boy in the Bush;* the Czechoslovakian count of "The Ladybird"; Lewis, the Welsh groom in *St. Mawr;* and Cipriano, the Indian general of *The Plumed Serpent.* These thin, bearded, and potent men, however, appear thinner, beardless, and impotent beside Mellors, gamekeeper to Lord Chatterley and symbol of Lawrence's dreams. This creature, who pleases the fruity, baronial Lady C., seems at first blush to be imperfectly qualified for so much happiness. He is the son of a miner, he seems to be unwell, and he has a cough. But his strength, his endurance, and his pleasures are almost incredible. "And what a reckless devil the man was!" thinks Lady Chatterley, "really like a devil! One had to be strong to bear him." [10]

Lawrence's discontent with the physical led him to improve the physical by fancy, but it also led him to the metaphysical. His hatred of the world, to which he could not adapt himself, and his efforts to find a cure for his troubles assumed a religious character. After 1915, when his troubles became too great to support, his life began to seem a crusade, each novel or essay a sermon, his person prophetical. To understand Lawrence's attitude toward Susan it is not enough to know that Susan is a natural, if not inevitable, result of the nerves and the discontent which drove Lawrence for comfort to extraordinary refuges. It is also necessary to examine his religious inclination and to follow it from its origin through its development to its riper state.

The religious impulse which elevates all that Lawrence did or said after the first year of the war had its origin in

[10] *Lady Chatterley's Lover,* p. 298.

his nature and found a suitable place to develop among the coal pits. In his town, religion took three regular courses: Church of England and two chapels, one of which was Primitive Methodist, the other Congregational. Most of the miners knew the Unknowable on Sundays and Tuesday nights in the Pentecost Methodist Chapel. Here their knowledge could grow without that questioning of divine justice which the presence of superior people might inspire, and their enthusiasm could spread without impediment; for superior and sober people attended Church or the other chapel according to their degree. From its foundation in the early years of the nineteenth century the sect of Primitive Methodists had offered revivals, enthusiasm, and social comfort to the lower orders of Nottinghamshire. Lawrence's grandfather had been an elder of a chapel in Nottingham, and his father, who sometimes sang in the choir, seems to have been a member of this communion at Eastwood, though his attendance at services after his marriage was inconstant. Lawrence's mother, a superior person, considered the Methodists, as well as her husband, common; and so she sent her children to her own chapel, the Congregational. She was puritanical and devout. Her children attended services three times every Sunday. They joined the Christian Endeavour and the Band of Hope. In their Sunday School class they were inflated by a blacksmith. They signed the pledge and intemperately sang "There's a Serpent in the Glass."

But for Lawrence this was not enough. While his mother's eyes were fixed on purity and truth of a Tuesday evening, he would go to the Methodist chapel with the miners, as he tells us in *Apocalypse*. At these services he was impressed with "an odd sense of wild mystery or . . . of rude power from above," [11] wanting among the sober Congregationalists. He attended revival meetings, which he used to burlesque in later years for the diversion of Frieda, and he was familiar with a "fervently evangelical *Life of John Wesley*." [12] That Lawrence was deeply impressed with the emotional, proletarian Methodists is apparent from the number of his references to them in his conversation and writing. From these remarks and perhaps from his conduct or manner Frieda and the Brewsters took it for granted that Lawrence had been a Methodist, and Ford Madox Ford, who says that Lawrence accompanied him to a service at the Methodist chapel of Eastwood, was sure of it. E. T. and Ada Lawrence, however, insist in their memoirs on Lawrence's Congregationalism and fail to mention the Methodists. The fact seems to be that although Lawrence was officially a Congregationalist, he was spiritually more at home among the Methodists, whom his snobbishness would not let him openly embrace. His occasional sneers at Methodism may be explained by his habit of tempering his attitudes to the taste of his auditors, when he thought them to be superior people, and by his habit of condemning what he liked.

Between the chapel of his mother and that of his fathers, Lawrence grew to be, if not a good Methodist or Congregationalist, a good Protestant. He had the Bible in his bones, as he tells us in *Apocalypse*:

[11] *Apocalypse*, p. 14.
[12] *The Tales of D. H. Lawrence*, p. 51.

From earliest years right into manhood, like any other non-conformist child I had the Bible poured every day into my helpless consciousness, till there came almost a saturation point. Long before one could think or even vaguely understand, this Bible language, these "portions" of the Bible were *douched* over the mind and consciousness, till they became soaked in, they became an influence which affected all the processes of emotion and thought.[13]

The hymns of the chapel also "penetrated through and through" his childish mind, filling it with wonder, as he tells us in his essay "Hymns in a Man's Life." This saturation with Bible and hymnal was not limited to his residence among the pits, for he continued to attend chapel every Sunday while at the teachers' college in Nottingham. It is not surprising that in later life his bones sang in accents of the chapel and that, like Ezekiel, Lawrence was able to prophesy upon these bones.

At college, however, and perhaps for a year or two before he went there, his bones were silent except for an occasional sigh. The chapel, though attended, ceased to be a rock of ages as the cleft in which Lawrence used to hide himself became first a serious fissure, then a geological fault. For he had begun to read the scientists, the materialists, and the rationalists of the nineteenth century, to whom rocks were rocks and chapels less than rocks. E. T., who knew Lawrence throughout this period, tells us what he read. He was fascinated by Darwin's *Origin of Species,* Huxley's *Man's Place in Nature,* Haeckel's *Riddle of the Universe,* and works by Herbert Spencer, John Stuart Mill, Hegel, and William James. Lawrence concluded not only that science and chapel

[13] Page 3; cf. *Phoenix, the Posthumous Papers of D. H. Lawrence,* p. 302.

could not be reconciled but that science was the truth and the way. He began fashionably to call himself an agnostic and was on the point of revealing the truth to the Congregational minister; but, dissuaded, he contented himself with lecturing a few years later to the socialist club at Croydon. This lecture, which has been printed in the memoir of Lawrence by Ada, his sister, invokes the names of Darwin, Spencer, Hegel, Mill.

Lawrence boasted while at college, and later, that he had ceased to be a Christian. But he had forgotten his bones, which remained protestant in both senses of the word. He was uncomfortable under a doctrine which might stimulate his mind but which left his emotions without support. Reason compelled skepticism; emotion demanded faith. For several years, as his mind disported itself, he gloomily contemplated the deserts of materialism. E. T. tells with what misery he observed the irreverence of those among whom he counted himself. At first unconsciously, and then consciously, he came to hate the science which had destroyed his belief. He could not return to the simple religion of his youth, yet he could not be content without religion. "Give us a religion," he said, "give us something to believe in, cries the unsatisfied soul embedded in the womb of our times." [14] There was only one thing to do and he did it: he invented a private religion.

The invention of a private belief as a substitute for an orthodox belief was not unusual among enlightened Protestants in the late nineteenth and the early twentieth centuries. After Darwin and Huxley, acceptance of the

[14] *Phoenix,* p. 434.

Christian miracles and forms became impossible for many men of religious temper and training. Incapable of happiness under materialism, they were forced to find an outlet for their emotions in a private or substitute belief. Lawrence falls, to the historian's delight, into a large pattern made by identical forces bearing on similar tempers.

The cases of Samuel Butler, Yeats, Shaw, and several other writers are like that of Lawrence. Butler was educated for the Anglican ministry, but he encountered doubts about the value of baptism. These doubts were followed by unbelief after he had read the Higher Criticism of the Germans and Darwin's *Origin of Species*. For a time he was a follower of Darwin, defending him against the attacks of a bishop. Butler's religious temper and training, however, made him unhappy as a materialist. After a few years he turned in rage against Darwin and, with the aid of Lamarck, who seemed to admit intelligence, desire, and design, wrote four unreadable books against materialism and chance in favor of the life-force. The acceptance of Butler's private religion by Bernard Shaw did less to prove its value than to make it semiprivate. The case of William Butler Yeats is even more striking than that of Samuel Butler or of his disciple. "I am very religious," said Yeats, "and deprived by Huxley and Tyndall, whom I detested, of the simple-minded religion of my childhood, I . . . made a new religion, almost an infallible church of poetic tradition . . ." [15] Yeats's excellent poetry came out of his

[15] *Autobiographies* (New York, Macmillan, 1927), p. 142.

private religion; but the works of Butler, Shaw, A.E., Herbert Read, and many others came out of theirs. Science and the religious temper, which have much to answer for, must also answer for this.

The religious temper seems to be native to many men. It is they who have found the age of science so difficult, and to their flight from materialism we must attribute the character of much modern art. That Lawrence had the religious temper is plain from the character of his works and from his own statements. "You should see," he said, "the religious, earnest, suffering man in me first." [16] "I always feel as if I stood naked for the fire of Almighty God to go through me—and it's rather an awful feeling. One has to be so terribly religious, to be an artist." [17] His concern with the soul, with its rushings to and from the Beyond, with the Unknown, and with the Infinite, which in a more suitable time might have made him a saint and perhaps a martyr, made him in ours a novelist.

His native enthusiasm, which made it impossible for him to remain a materialist, was improved by the chapel. The private religion of his later years seems to owe much to enthusiastic Methodism. *Apocalypse,* one of the principal testaments of his faith, was inspired, in part at least, by the interest of the miners in the Book of Revelation and by his own youthful immersion in that mystery. Throughout his life he was accustomed, in his essays and letters, to translate his private fancies into the imagery

[16] *Letters,* p. 190.
[17] *Ibid.,* p. 109. Cf. *The Boy in the Bush,* p. 355: Jack's nature is "emotionally mystical."

and diction of the Scriptures.[18] The puritanism as well as the language of the chapel remained with him, but, inverted and applied to different objects, it seemed singular to other puritans. The author of *Lady Chatterley's Lover,* who considered *Ulysses* indecent, need not have been at such pains to declare himself in several passionate essays and pamphlets an adorer of the pure. No one but a puritan could have written *Lady Chatterley;* nor could any but a nonconformist have devised a religion like Lawrence's. In his pursuit of individual judgment and of immediate communion with God, Lawrence was following the nonconformist way, which leads logically to the private faith with its freedom from the restraints of custom and discipline. Dissatisfied with his sect, the Protestant may join a more congenial sect or walk alone. Before the time of Darwin the lonely walk was generally Christian; in Lawrence's time generally not, but it was still Protestant.

Lawrence's Protestant departure from the Christian way led to strange places and stranger notions. But his first gropings after that in which he could believe were normal enough. Before he had entirely abandoned Christianity for materialism, he had been attracted to idealists, transcendentalists, and unorthodox enthusiasts. He read Kant; he liked Emerson, Thoreau, Wordsworth, and Whitman; and he adored Shelley, Carlyle, and Blake. In these he recognized an affinity, and later on he found in them some compensation for the loss of Methodism as well as some relief from the tedium of science.

[18] The mind of Jack Grant of *The Boy in the Bush* is filled, like his creator's, with Scripture images (pp. 2, 153). This novel is an elaborate variation upon the Cain-Abel theme.

Pantheism and the doctrine of the Oversoul, which he may have found in Emerson, Thoreau, or Wordsworth, were his first refuge from materialism. In 1911 he wrote a letter to his sister, describing God as

a vast shimmering impulse which waves onwards towards some end. . . . When we die, like rain-drops falling back again into the sea, we fall back into the big, shimmering sea of unorganized life which we call God. We are lost as individuals, yet we count in the whole. It requires a lot of pain and courage to come to discover one's own creed, and quite as much to continue in lonely faith. Would you like a book or two of philosophy? or will you merely battle out your own ideas? I would still go to chapel if it did me any good. . . . It is a fine thing to establish one's own religion in one's heart, not to be dependent on tradition and second-hand ideals.[19]

This letter shows his earliest efforts to create a "lonely faith," and in the reference to books of philosophy it also shows another source upon which he had begun to draw.

The philosophers who appealed most to him in the period between college and the war seem to have been the Greeks, not Aristotle, but Plato and, still more, the earlier men like Herakleitos and Anaximander, in whose notions of flow, of balance, and of the elements [20] it is evident that he found much comfort. By 1915 he had gone through the Greeks and had proceeded to higher heights and deeper depths. "I shall write all my philosophy again," he says in a letter of 1915. "Last time I came out of the Christian Camp. This time I must come out of

[19] Ada Lawrence and G. Stuart Gelder, *Early Life of D. H. Lawrence,* pp. 72–73.
[20] For the source of Lawrence's knowledge of the early Greeks see *infra,* Chapter IV.

those early Greek philosophers. I am so sure of what I know, and what is true." [21] This rewritten philosophy, of which he was so sure, is the second stage in the development of his private religion. From the apocalyptic essays he wrote at this time for *The Signature,* we may gather that in this stage his philosophy retained fragments of the Greek fragments together with traces of the chapel, but Lawrence's philosophy in this stage is significant only of his confusion. That it satisfied him as little as it does the critical reader is plain from its further development. By the end of the war, after much reading and after the addition of many new elements, his religion emerged complete, many-sided, and very private.

The first new element of this religion was a theory of relationship, mindlessness, and blood as the way of salvation. The second was a theory of the primitive, especially the animism and the conduct of pious barbarians, as the pattern for modern man to follow. The third was the occult, particularly theosophy and yoga, which from 1915 onwards smoothed Lawrence's path to the Infinite.[22] Blood, mindlessness, and relationship were also and more conveniently known to him as love or power. "The real power," said he, "comes in to us from beyond. Life enters us from behind . . ." [23] To Lawrence, who could see beyond the behind, love was a bridge between the flesh and the spirit, like animism and theosophy. Love, primitivism, and the occult superseded, but did

---

[21] *Letters,* p. 235.

[22] "Identity with the infinite," he said, "is the goal of life." *Phoenix,* p. 615.

[23] *Reflections on the Death of a Porcupine,* p. 152.

not destroy all trace of, Emerson, the Methodists, and the Greeks.

The next chapters will deal with the origin and nature of these elements of his metaphysics together with their literary manifestations. Before proceeding to these matters, however, we must consider Lawrence's idea of himself as the priest and his works as the sermons of his religion.

"I shall always be a priest of love," said Lawrence, ". . . and I'll preach my heart out." [24] Priest and preacher, however, are descriptions too mild to fit one who in his own and in his disciples' eyes was hero, prophet, and even saviour. Of the hero, Lawrence said: "I do think that man is related to the universe in some 'religious' way, even prior to his relation to his fellow man. . . . There is a *principle* in the universe, towards which man turns religiously—a *life* of the universe itself. And the hero is he who touches and transmits the life of the universe." [25] In his capacity of prophet, the hero teaches man to open his heart to the mysterious flow of power and glory from the Unseen, the Unknown, the Beyond.[26] In his capacity of saviour, he puts man into a new relationship with God. God is always the same, said Lawrence, but new times and new people need new saviours. Observing the fall of saviours as of sparrows, God sends a new saviour where and when he is needed. Lawrence saw the need was great; he seems to have thought that God had called and that the call had come to him.[27]

[24] *Letters*, p. 88. [25] *Ibid.*, p. 688. [26] *Porcupine*, pp. 152–53, 184.
[27] *Ibid.*, pp. 228–29, 237–38; *Phoenix*, pp. 727, 729.

As we have seen, the typical hero of his fiction combined what Lawrence was and what he thought he was
with what he would like to be. These heroes give us a
clearer idea of his nature and desires than we can get
from his letters. Birkin, the hero of *Women in Love,* is
Lawrence as prophet and saviour, a leader with new values come to save the world with a "new gospel." As
prophet he condemns what he is about to save and announces: " 'I believe in the unseen hosts!' " After one
of his sermons on Sodom, Ursula sees he is a saviour, a
preacher, and a prophet but, unconverted as yet, dis-
likes him in these capacities: "She wanted him to herself,
she hated the Salvator Mundi touch." Lawrence had detected a similar attitude in Frieda, who, he complained,
had no use for the Infinite.[28] More potent than his creator, however, Birkin is finally able to persuade his pedestrian mate to leave the ground and fly with him. From
their elevation they despise the sneers of the irreverent
and the blind, who are represented in this novel by the
Bohemians of Bloomsbury. These wastrels, at their table
in a restaurant, read and ridicule one of Birkin's proph-
ecies, which " 'almost supersedes the Bible.' " Of Birkin
one says: " 'He makes me perfectly sick. He is as bad as
Jesus. Lord, *what* must I do to be saved!' " Another says:
" 'Of course, it is a form of religious mania. He thinks he
is the Saviour of man . . .' " Birkin's gospel that desire
is holy, that savages are good, and that the Mindless and
the Infinite are the way and the end of salvation receives
the malice and the ridicule of these bad men.[29] Law-

[28] *Letters,* pp. 239–40; cf. Mrs. Somers in *Kangaroo,* p. 195.
[29] *Women in Love,* pp. 59, 60, 145, 146, 300, 437–41. Cf. *Kangaroo,*
p. 277: Somers feels like a "crucified Christ" when he does not feel like

rence's occasional ability to see himself as others saw
him did not alter his flight or ground him; for he saw
with approval what they saw with malice, and, carried
even higher by the heat of their contempt than by that
of his enthusiasm, he continued to prophesy and to make
prophetical heroes in his own image. Lilly, the hero of
Aaron's Rod, preaches destruction and salvation and sees
himself surrounded by Judases: " 'Well, if one will be a
Jesus,' " he says in a moment of bitterness, " 'he must expect his Judas. . . . A Jesus makes a Judas inevitable.' "
The ingratitude of his disciples is almost enough to make
Lilly exchange the role of saviour for that of private
citizen and to leave the world to the mercies of "mechanical doctors and nurses." [30] Such qualms, however, never
impair the constancy of Don Ramon, hero of *The
Plumed Serpent,* the saviour of saviours, who sees his efforts revive a nation, who sees and indeed effects the destruction of the wicked, and through whom love, power,
and glory well from the past to make the world a better
place for Lawrence to live in.

These fancies were shared and applauded by the disciples. In her more hopeful moods Mrs. Luhan saw
Lawrence as a Jesus; in her less hopeful, as a John the
Baptist. The Honorable Dorothy Brett painted a cruci-
fixion in which Jesus wears beneath His crown of thorns
the face of Lawrence. This picture was intended not to
reveal or to increase the passion of the old Saviour but
to reveal and increase that of the new. The editor of
The Phoenix, a Laurentian quarterly, founded in 1938

an ordinary martyr; see p. 70 for Somers as saviour, p. 140 for Kangaroo
as rival saviour.

[30] *Aaron's Rod,* pp. 113–14, 342–44.

and issued at Woodstock, New York, and Paris, France, insists that Lawrence is a saviour, whose message, far deeper than that of Hitler, points the way for fallen man to follow.

Lawrence's messianic character appears best, however, at the dinner he gave to his disciples at the Café Royal in 1923 before his second coming to New Mexico. The accounts of this dinner fall naturally into the imagery of the Last Supper and the Betrayal. According to the Honorable Dorothy Brett, Lawrence remarked on this occasion: " 'I am not a man. . . . I am Man.' " [31] That is an interesting point, but it is to Mrs. Carswell that we owe the fullest history of this unfortunate repast. She says that Lawrence asked each of the disciples in turn to forsake the world and go with him to Taos and the new dispensation. The Honorable Dorothy Brett and Mrs. Carswell (although she did not have the fare) agreed to go; some jestingly complied; but the others denied him. Middleton Murry, as he did so, arose and, according to Mrs. Carswell, kissed Lawrence. " 'Women can't understand this,' " Mr. Murry is said to have said. " 'Maybe,' " replied Mrs. Carswell, " 'but anyhow it wasn't a woman who betrayed Jesus with a kiss.' " Turning to Lawrence, Mr. Murry is said to have said, " 'I *have* betrayed you, old chap, I confess it.' " Lawrence put his head on the table and vomited. The disciples, including Judas, raised "the limp figure of their master" and took him home. [32]

[31] *Lawrence and Brett,* p. 21.
[32] Catherine Carswell, *The Savage Pilgrimage,* pp. 209–13; cf. *Letters,* p. 628. For Mr. Murry's account of this occasion see *Son of Woman,* pp. 310–12, 366. Mr. Murry is correct in considering Lawrence a prophet rather than an artist.

It was fortunate for his self-esteem that Lawrence could endure the role of saviour without a smile. Not that he never laughed: he was given to boisterous levity, to horseplay, and to pranks such as painting flowers and serpents on Mr. Luhan's garden house. All the memoirs agree on Lawrence's high spirits, and Lawrence endowed his Birkin with irresponsible gaiety. "I don't take myself seriously," said Lawrence, "except between 8.0 and 10.0 a.m., and at the stroke of midnight." [33] But Lawrence and his friends were deceived; for beneath his superficial levity he was a very solemn man at any hour. He had neither detachment nor humor. His nature is less apparent in his pranks than in his hatred of levity and irreverence in others, in his detestation of rival saviours—to whom he was indebted, but who deviated in particulars from Laurentian orthodoxy—and in his endurance of the disciples. Nature and circumstance, which had denied him much, gave him solemnity, the gift he needed to support his part.

In his role of prophet Lawrence played Jeremiah and Noah to an inattentive house. Like the Birkins and Lillys of his novels, he damned the times in which he was unable to be happy and gloomily predicted sorrow for others. In this exercise he found a natural as well as a prophetical pleasure. The modern world, he announced, was dead and corrupted, and before it died it had killed the soul. He called in vain for an earthquake, a revolution, a flood to kill what he had found dead and to restore the soul to its home in the Infinite. At times he thought the flood he prayed for might come and he ex-

[33] *Letters*, p. 645.

claimed: "What one needs is an ark." [34] In his less nautical moods, as he fled from Sodom he turned his head for a final look and remained petrified where he stood, a pillar of salty but by no means silent dismay.

In his role of saviour, Lawrence emerged from his ark or abandoned the position of Lot's wife and descended to the cities of the plain. The citizens of Sodom and Gomorrah, he said, were in the tomb, but if they listened to him, they would find that the present time was merely the interval between Good Friday and Easter.[35] Rebirth, resurrection, the reincarnation of the Phoenix, the emergence into the Greater Day, and many other profitable things would come to those who acknowledged his gospel. This interest in rebirth is not odd in one who had been raised in the chapel, but it might seem odd in one who, referring to the revival meetings of the Methodists, said he had a horror of being saved. It is more natural, however, for a saviour to save than to be saved.

Jeremiah was hoarse and Noah was disappointed by the refusal of a passport when in 1915 Lawrence the saviour commenced to save. With the aid of Bertrand Russell, he planned to establish a religious order in London around the conception of "the reality of the clear, eternal spirit." From this center they would create by their preaching a new heaven and a new earth. This might seem an extravagant hope, but Lawrence said: "One must put away all ordinary common sense, I think,

[34] *Ibid.*, pp. 652, 667; cf. the symbolical flood which destroys the evils of the present in *The Virgin and the Gipsy: Tales*, p. 1091.
[35] *Letters*, p. 687. See his poem on resurrection and rebirth: "New Heaven and Earth," *Collected Poems*, II, 97.

and work only from the invisible world." The preachers, however, could not get together. Russell wanted to lecture on politics; Lawrence rejected this worldliness with contempt. He wanted the Infinite, the Boundless, the Eternal as a starting point, whence he could proceed to speak his "soul's words"; for, as he said, "to have to speak in the body is a violation to me." But Russell didn't want the Infinite, Lawrence escaped violation, and the religious center came to nothing.[36]

There was still another hope, however, in the religious magazine *The Signature* which Lawrence and Murry published during that same year. Here Lawrence could print the sermons he had not been permitted to preach. For this magazine he wrote "The Crown" and several other metaphorical exhortations, which make his enthusiasm and his desire to save clearer than what he had to say. To the worldly mind these effusions seem lyrical and obscure; to Lawrence they seemed "very beautiful and very good. I feel if only people, decent people, would read them, somehow a new era might set in." Of the magazine itself he said: "It is really *something:* the seed, I hope, of a great change in life: the beginning of a new religious era, from my point. I hope to God the new religious era is starting into being also at other points, and that soon there will be a body of believers, in this howling desert of unbelief and sensation." [37] *The Signature* had thirty subscribers.

The disappointed saviour did not abandon hope. He continued to plan religious centers in Florida, Taos, Mexico, and England, but his hopes of founding and

[36] *Letters,* pp. 239–60.   [37] *Ibid.,* pp. 258–60.

directing his own community were never fulfilled. His inability to get along with other men, his insistence that Russell and Murry accept his ideas and defer to his leadership as disciples to master postponed the rebirth of the world indefinitely.

If he could not lead, he could write, and his novels became the only outlet for his zeal. "Primarily I am a passionately religious man," he said, "and my novels must be written from the depth of my religious experience . . ." [38] From this depth his novels received, and all but burst with, his message to the world; they were written with an energy and purpose which would have been expended better perhaps in a religious community or in Hyde Park. Had Bertrand Russell been less stubborn, Lawrence's novels might have been more than sermons. But literature's loss was philosophy's gain.

[38] *Ibid.*, p. 190.

CHAPTER TWO

NEVER MIND

M Y great religion," said Lawrence, mistaking the part for the whole, "is a belief in the blood, the flesh, as being wiser than the intellect." [1] Bloody rebellion against the intellect was only the negative side of his religion, as intolerance of Russia is the negative side of an archdeacon's, but it occupied Lawrence's nights and days and became a theme of his fiction. His crusade against the world singled out for attack the foundations of modern society: reason, science, materialism, and the machine. In the role of Noah he fled these; in the role of Jeremiah he damned them. But the prophet was pleased with Susan whose blood flowed, as her milk, without impediment of mind; for she had no mind. "She doesn't even know me," gloated the enemy of knowledge.

She doesn't know that I am a gentleman on two feet. Not she. Something mysterious happens in her blood and her being, when she smells me and my nice white trousers. . . . She comes to, out of a sort of trance, and is relieved, trotting up home with a queer, jerky cowy gladness. . . . Where she is when she's *in* the trance, heaven only knows. That's Susan! I have a certain relation to her.[2]

This perfect animal naturally became the object of his devotion and the symbol of the good.

Mindlessness had not always been Lawrence's ideal. E. T. says that Lawrence once considered himself an in-

[1] *Letters,* p. 94.   [2] *Porcupine,* pp. 166–67.

tellectual, that he despised her for being a creature of emotion, and that before the sudden end of their acquaintance he had told her that he could understand women only with his mind. This was during his college days, however, while he fancied himself a materialist, before his meeting with Frieda and the development of his religion. By 1913 he had become an enemy of what he called sometimes intellect, sometimes mind. "All I want," he exclaimed in this year, "is to answer to my blood, direct, without fribbling intervention of mind . . ." [3] He believed mind to be sterile and abominable, ideas and abstractions to be a kind of mildew, and logic to be too crude to deal with life. With knowledge and self-consciousness, he said, came the Fall, and he longed for the days before the Fall, before mental consciousness had become the director of man. In his ark, from which he thought he had pumped or jettisoned all intellect, he announced the joy of "mindless animation," of living the dark life from centers deeper than the brain, from blood, bowels, lungs, and liver, but not lights. [4]

He saw that, except for a clinical interest in laboratory or sickroom, these dark centers were ignored by fallen man. Civilization had succumbed to science, the least attractive form and way of knowledge. It was accordingly for science that Lawrence reserved his severest censure. We have seen that he had been a reader of Darwin and Huxley; and when he was a teacher at Croydon, he had received the praise of the overseers for excellence at

---

[3] *Letters*, p. 94.

[4] *Psychoanalysis and the Unconscious*, pp. 120–22, 126–27; *Phoenix*, pp. 29, 249–50, 299, 644, 766–67; *Letters*, pp. 94, 183, 300; *Porcupine*, pp. 64, 207; *Kangaroo*, p. 231.

science. Once elevated by the spirit and convinced of the hollowness of materialism, however, he was enabled by his experience of evil to take arms more cunningly against it and to find the vulnerable spots. To his proclamation of the worthlessness of mind he added an exposure of the worthlessness of science. He could not tolerate the idea of fixed, mechanical law, the "bunk of geology, and strata, and . . . biology or evolution," or the substitution of H_2O for the naïve, potable element. Jonathan Swift had objected to scientists because he thought them unreasonable; Lawrence objected to them because he thought them reasonable. "Man is not a little engine of cause and effect," he said, nor is the sun of heaven a ball of blazing gas as men of science would have us believe, but a living mystery as savages and Chaldeans knew. "I would rather listen now to a negro witch-doctor," said Lawrence, "than to Science." [5]

Psychoanalysis and the Unconscious, first published in 1921, is the most complete early expression of this attitude. In this work he uses Freud as a symbol of the scientist, a man who is logical, bound by the laws of cause and effect, and ignorant of mystery. But Einstein, who is perhaps a more considerable scientist than Freud, appealed to Lawrence because he had used the word "relativity," which Lawrence liked, and because he had done so much to destroy the logical universe of the nineteenth century. In *Movements in European History* Lawrence condemned the scientific historian, who imposes a logical cause and effect pattern upon those unreasonable

[5] *Porcupine*, p. 129; *Fantasia of the Unconscious*, pp. 136–37; cf. *Phoenix*, pp. 298–300, 528, 535, 757; *Apocalypse*, p. 168; *Assorted Articles*, p. 23; *Kangaroo*, pp. 330–31.

surges in the souls of men to which Lawrence the historian, dispensing with logic and cause, and reverent of mysteries, promised to be faithful. He detected the smell of science and logic even in current art, such as the work of Marinetti the futurist, Arnold Bennett, H. G. Wells, James Joyce, and, oddly, the French symbolists. He called Ibsen, Flaubert, and Hardy "the Nihilists, the intellectual, hopeless people," from whose error he hoped mankind was now escaping by way of a religious revival. It is time, he said in 1913, for a revolt against Shaw and Galsworthy, "the rule and measure mathematical folk." [6]

Science was most evident, however, not in works of art but in the machine, upon which Lawrence seized as the symbol of what is wrong with the world. All things have a vital relationship with one another, he said, except the machine, which is "absolutely material and absolutely anti-physical," destitute of "life-contact." The thought of wheels and engines made him miserable. He recoiled from the thought that the earth turns like a wheel, denying it vehemently and insisting that the earth turns with a vital, hovering flight, not to be understood. For he loved the earth, as he hated the world, and he fled for relief to flowers and trees, in which he found no wheels. The heroine of *Women in Love,* who shares her creator's feelings, exclaims: " 'No flowers grow upon busy machinery . . .' ".[7]

---

[6] *Letters,* pp. 103, 119, 196; *Phoenix,* p. 304; cf. *Psychoanalysis,* pp. 19, 22–26, 32–34, and *Fantasia,* p. 20.

[7] *Women in Love,* p. 219; *Assorted Articles,* p. 144; cf. *Porcupine,* p. 235, and *Phoenix,* pp. 26–28, 31, 590, 611, 618, 631. See poems against machines, machine society, and abstractions: *Last Poems,* pp. 47–55, 126, 153, 165, 168, 178, 187, 191, 194, 196. As Lawrence observes in *Twilight in Italy,* p. 72: "It is a . . . horrible thing to see tigers caught up and entangled and torn in machinery."

The words mechanical, automatic, and materialistic became Lawrence's epithets of abuse. He applied them indifferently to mind, logic, science, and machines. Against the age of mechanism and materialism he directed sermon after sermon, sometimes in the form of essays, sometimes of novels, sometimes of poems, each more spiritual than the last, each a more potent antidote to mind. Since he was more at home in the novel than in the essay, we must turn to his novels for his less unreadable sermons against the materialists. A survey of this ever-recurring theme in his fiction is as important to a study of this sort as it promises to be obvious, repetitious, and tiresome. But the reader of Lawrence, accustomed to the ways of his author, cannot but delight in it.

The characters in the novels and stories of Lawrence's middle and later periods are allegorical, designed to teach moral and spiritual lessons by their nature, words, and conduct. Some represent the bad, some the good, all their creator's concern with mind and matter. Gerald, of *Women in Love,* is a bad man, a mine-owning materialist, whose head contains "a million wheels and cogs and axles." This mechanical man, for whom nothing remains but death, slips a cog one day on an Alp; but before he perishes he translates "Godhead into mechanism," hardens the hearts of the miners, and dims the light of love in their eyes by introducing American machinery in place of the more natural shovel.

It was the first great step in undoing, the first great phase of chaos, the substitution of the mechanical principle for the organic, the destruction of the organic purpose, the organic unity, and the subordination of every organic unit to the great mechanical purpose. It was pure organic disintegration and pure mechanical organization.[8]

Gudrun exclaims, " 'What weariness, God above!' " and recoils from this man of wheels to another better adapted to her purposes. She has previously rejected a suitor because he is a scientist. But Hermione is an unnatural creature. Without dark spontaneity, "full of intellectuality, and heavy, nerve-worn with consciousness," she gives week-end parties of a "mental and very wearying" sort. Ursula and Birkin, who continually preach and sometimes experience the joys of mindlessness, flee with horror from her parties. They are unable to regard the trees with indifference, nor can they let the flowers alone. Count Psanek, the little black hero of "The Ladybird," shares their inabilities. He wants to destroy the factories, leaving only the birds and the trees and himself crooning mindlessly; for he has a low brow and a dark soul. His crooning seems a call from the Beyond to Daphne, who is wafted away beyond the world, her "darkness answering to darkness, and deep answering to deep." The Count's arrival in her home has proved a happy release; her husband is a very mental man.

Husbands, fathers, mine-owners, and vicars generally serve in these allegories as representatives of the mind and the machine, from which their wives or daughters are freed by the aid of grooms, gamekeepers, gipsies, crooners, or horses. Rico, the husband of the heroine of *St. Mawr,* is described as all head, a machine in a world where men are little motorcars. From this husband and

8 *Women in Love,* p. 263.

this world the heroine escapes by the aid of Phoenix, a redskin groom who cannot stand or even understand logical speech, of Lewis a Welsh groom with animal intelligence, intuitions, and a mystery about him, and of St. Mawr a horse. The important daughter in the "Daughters of the Vicar" and the virgin in *The Virgin and the Gipsy* escape their mechanical fathers by the aid of a coal miner and a gipsy. Everyone knows what distraction from her intellectual, mine-owning, powerless husband Lady Chatterley finds in the keeper of her husband's game.

The flight from mind and machine on the part of his heroines was well enough, but Lawrence appears to have discovered even more pleasure in the destruction of the machine by his hero Don Ramon in *The Plumed Serpent.* This dark saviour sees that the souls of the Mexicans have been oppressed by the machines and factories introduced into the land of Quetzalcoatl by pale men from the north. For a time he contents himself with sermons on cogwheels, but when this fails to move the materialists, he arises, seizes the church, stops the clock in its tower, abolishes mechanical time, and uses the drum to mark the watches of the natural day. After this symbolical triumph of soul over machine, he closes the factories, and the spirit of Mexico is saved from materialism. The Utopia of Quetzalcoatl was a more perfect refuge for Lawrence's fancy than the park of Lord Chatterley in which the glare of the neighboring pits disturbs the spiritual exercises of the refugees.

Lawrence's campaign against materialism supplied the plots, or at least a principal theme, of these and many other stories, which it would be tedious to number. It also supplied much of the symbolism to be found in these allegories. The horse, for example, figures in many of Lawrence's works as the symbol of the dark unmechanical spirit. In *Women in Love* Gerald brutally compels his mare to face a locomotive at the railway crossing. The reluctant beast, her rider, and the busy, inorganic engine symbolize the soul forced by will and mind to endure civilization. Charlie Chaplin caught in the gears of the enormous machine during lunch hour is a similar and no less happy conceit. Though Mr. Chaplin will do to symbolize the plight of man, the horse is a better symbol of the soul's discomfort and, since it is a beast, more suitable for pointing the dark way to freedom. It is as a symbol of this way that St. Mawr is used, and as a device for revealing the presence of soul in the people of the story. Those who are blood-conscious or soulful, like Lewis and the heroine, understand the animal; those who are mental, like Rico, hate him. Not only horses but cows, cats, and fishes appear as symbols in the other books. The park in *Lady Chatterley* is as symbolic as the paralysis of its owner. Even his wheelchair is a symbol of the machine. As this little engine chuffs through the park it crushes flowers with its cruel wheels.

The evils of mind, matter, and machines never appear in Lawrence's stories without indication of their remedies, some of which have been mentioned by the way. In place of these evils Lawrence proposed, as we have seen, a return to nature. He also proposed what he called soul, love, blood-consciousness, the unconscious, the organic, the dynamic, and the vital, which, as we shall see, are names for the same thing. These names and this thing are mysterious and profound, not to be understood but to be felt. By their nature they provided Lawrence and his readers with another cure for the mental and the clear. To understand his cures we must first contemplate mystery and depth, in themselves a cure and the quality of the others.

Lawrence liked what he could not understand because he could not understand it. He rejected engines and syllogisms, which he could follow or at least approach with his understanding, for the unthinkable. "All the best part of knowledge," he said in *Psychoanalysis and the Unconscious,* "is inconceivable." [9] Civilized man, he complained, has cut himself off from mystery and, as his hero Birkin adds, " 'doesn't embody the utterance of the incomprehensible any more . . .' " [10] Instead of trying to conquer or to conceive the world and instead of trying to reduce life to engine, man should abandon himself to "mindless progressive knowledge through the senses . . . mystical knowledge," [11] to fluid darkness, and to mystery; for it is only on wonder, the natural religious sense, that man can thrive. Lawrence's heroes and heroines thrive. After having approached the daisy for years with the eye of the botanist, Ursula finds relief in "mystical" contemplation of that blossom and like her tutor, Birkin, turns from botany to "the unseen hosts" behind the flowers. Wonder, mystery, and the "mystical"—these delight Lawrence's creatures, who also feel, not from intellectual pride but from its opposite, that what they cannot understand must be

[9] Page 42.   [10] *Women in Love,* p. 65.   [11] *Ibid.,* p. 289.

profound. Deep and dark are their favorite words, of which the hero of "Glad Ghosts," for example, is unable to resist the former:

It is even not himself, deep beyond his many depths. Deep from him calls to deep. And according as deep answers deep, man glistens and surpasses himself.

Beyond all the pearly mufflings of consciousness, of age upon age of consciousness, deep calls yet to deep, and sometimes is answered. It is calling and answering, new-awakened God calling within the deep of man, and new God calling answer from the other deep. And sometimes the other deep is a woman . . .[12]

Nothing is deeper than the unconscious, as Lawrence discovered in his rebellion against the intellect. He got the word unconscious and a notion of its meaning from Freud, but aside from its name Lawrence's unconscious was his own invention, assembled from non-Freudian materials. Lawrence first heard of Freud from Frieda at their first meeting, after he had written a draft of *Sons and Lovers,* and he heard more about Freud in Germany; but from Lawrence's references to psychoanalysis it is plain that his acquaintance with the subject remained casual. His unwillingness to pursue Freud's theory was natural since Freud seemed to him to be a scientist. But Lawrence gladly pursued his own theory in *Psychoanalysis and the Unconscious,* a work devoted to showing how superior his unconscious was to that of Freud. Freud's was logical, scientific, dead, Lawrence's the real thing.

Far from being the repository of complexes, said Lawrence, the unconscious is the soul. Indeed, soul would

[12] *Tales,* p. 896.

have been a better word for the unconscious, but he
was willing to retain Freud's word since the word soul
had been vitiated by the profane. This consideration,
however, rarely kept Lawrence or his heroes from using
the vitiated word. Birkin rebukes Gerald and Ursula
Hermione for neglecting the soul, and in Lawrence's
other novels and in his essays the word soul is second in
favor only to dark. Whatever its name, his unconscious
was a spiritual retreat from mind and world; but in his
conception of the spiritual Lawrence embraced more
than a clergyman would allow. He included the body
or at least the torso—a region, according to him, despised
by the clergy and the worldly alike. He liked to refer
to his unconscious by synecdoche as the blood or more
generally as the organic, which is opposite to the mechanical, and as the physical, which is opposite to the
material. Spiritual man was to him "a column of rapa-
cious and living blood." [13]

The unconscious, Lawrence announced in *Psychoanalysis and the Unconscious*, is inconceivable. But this
difficulty did not keep him from conceiving it, from
knowing his way about among the ganglia and the tripes,
or from charting these depths. He found that the unconscious is divided into four principal parts, the lumbar,
the thoracic, the cardiac, and the solar plexus. The last
part seemed the best, the furthest from mind, and the
most "pristine." These four centers, he said, are charged
with positive and negative electricity like batteries, and,
though dark and complicated, the circuits of force among
them and with external objects were neither too dark

[13] *Porcupine,* p. 117.

nor too complicated for him. *Psychoanalysis and the Unconscious* contains a detailed analysis, which may be reduced to diagram, of the elements and forces of the unconscious.

To the skeptic who might ask how Lawrence could know the unknowable, he replied that he knew what was what by the old religious faculty of intuition: "Religion was right and science is wrong." [14] For the way of the scientists and for their absurdities about sun, moon, and bowels, he had substituted "subjective science" based on the data of living experience. He could feel the truth. How all this was he did not know, but he knew it was so. Intuition, instinct, and impulse were better guides through the darkness than the blind, limited intellect. How fine it is, says Birkin, " 'to act spontaneously on one's impulses,' " and, he might have added, to think with one's blood.

Their reliance upon the impulses and the intuitions from their blood accounts for the irrational behavior of Lawrence's heroines. When they are at their best these people are unconscious or all but unconscious. Ursula, that "strange, unconscious bud of powerful womanhood," [15] is continually swooning with acute comprehension or succumbing to trances and transports, "gone into the ultimate darkness of her own soul." [16] Obeying an impulse from her unconscious, Gudrun dances before astonished cows. Her habit of wearing red, green, blue, or yellow stockings can be explained by neither fashion nor reason. The aim of the unconscious hero, however,

[14] *Psychoanalysis*, p. 41; cf. *Fantasia*, p. 8.
[15] *Women in Love*, p. 103. [16] *Ibid.*, p. 220.

is not merely to lose his mind but, as Lawrence points out in his *Fantasia of the Unconscious,* to practice religion and love, the deepest activities of the unconscious. The success of the first of these activities, said Lawrence, is dependent upon that of the second, and it is for—or partly for—the Greater Purpose that his heroes are always making love. Birkin and Don Cipriano spring from their beds to save the world. It is true that Mellors, the gamekeeper, rarely leaves his bed, but at least he is unconscious there.

Lawrence had a better word than soul for his unconscious: "The term unconscious," he said, "is only another word for life." [17] And life, as he never tired of saying, is relationship and flow. The words flux, dynamic, and relative had their place in Lawrence's vocabulary with soul, dark, organic, and blood. He discovered change and flow in what he liked, fixity in what he abhorred, even in the engine. Nothing was less dynamic to him than the dynamo. He knew that all living things such as heroes and vegetables constantly change in an "odd fluid relatedness." The hero is a wave in the creative flux, a fish in the stream, and in submitting to its flow is his peace. His solar plexus is dynamic, his mind is gone. Into such a man the life-force flows from behind, below, and beyond, filling him with power and connecting him vitally with sun and moon. It is then that "The sun of China and Mithras blazes over him and gives him not radiant energy in the form of heat and light, but life, life, life!" [18] The heroes of Lawrence's novels broil be-

[17] *Psychoanalysis,* pp. 108–9.
[18] *Porcupine,* p. 230; cf. pp. 23, 37–38, 114, 119, and also *Assorted*

neath this sun. Ursula is fascinated with Birkin's mysterious life-flow, which seems to have been identical with what Lawrence calls elsewhere "the flux of sap-consciousness." [19]

Lawrence had many names for the unconscious and there are many names for what Lawrence was, but at this place it is enough, perhaps, to call him a vitalist. As a worshiper of life he wanted a universe which was "alive and kicking" in place of the dead machine of matter and energy imagined by the scientists. He wanted life to supplant civilization, mind, and death. He wanted art to promote what he wanted. But he wanted art.

His formula for vital art, especially for the vitalist novel, is simple. The business of art, he said in his many essays on the novel, is to be true to flux and the living mystery. Of the arts the novel is the highest because the least capable of the absolute. The good novelist lets the wind of life blow through him and abandons himself to flow and change. Above all he avoids "fences" or formal patterns which impair the purity and check the impetuosity of the life-force. To Lawrence, Joyce and Proust were bad novelists because they were abstract, logical, formal, and ignorant of life. Harry Crosby, the poet, however, was good. In a review of his *Chariot of the Sun*, Lawrence praised Crosby for his disorder and vitality. Order, said Lawrence, is an umbrella hiding the sun; disorder in art opens the soul to chaos. And in a letter he said that he preferred chaos to abstraction

Articles, pp. 49–50; *Letters,* pp. 635, 638; *Phoenix,* pp. 525, 527–32, 670–74.

[19] *Psychoanalysis,* p. 48; cf. *Porcupine,* pp. 130, 149, 153, 176, 210.

and mechanical order. True to his principles of mind-lessness, but not without logic or consistency, he defined the good novel as a lively chaos.[20]

Chaos is the end but not the only way of the vital novelist. He may also achieve mindlessness and explore the living unconscious by means of myths and symbols. At the same time he may interest and instruct a wide audience since "for the mass of people knowledge must be symbolical, mythical, dynamic." [21] Lawrence defined and explained the value of myth and symbol in his Preface to Frederick Carter's *Dragon of the Alchemists:*

Symbols are organic units of consciousness with a life of their own, and you can never explain them away, because their value is dynamic, emotional, belonging to the sense-consciousness of the body and soul, and not simply mental. . . . Myth is an attempt to narrate a whole human experience, of which the purpose is too deep, going too deep in the blood and soul, for mental explanation or description. . . . And the images of myth are symbols. . . . A complex of emotional experience is a symbol. And the power of the symbol is to arouse the deep emotional self, and the dynamic self, beyond comprehension.[22]

These dynamic instruments, going too deep into blood and soul to be understood, seem to have been made for the use of the mindless vitalist. By their aid Lawrence hoped to express and recommend the inexpressible. For this reason, among others which will appear later, he delighted in the Aztec myth of Quetzalcoatl, in the myth of the Man Who Died, and in the occasional symbols of

[20] *Porcupine,* p. 121; *Phoenix,* pp. 255, 261, 517, 527–32; *Letters,* p. 605.
[21] *Fantasia,* p. 68.
[22] *Phoenix,* pp. 295–96. Cf. Lawrence's essay on Hawthorne in *The English Review,* XXVIII (May, 1919), 405: ". . . myth is most repugnant to reason."

horses and engines to be found in his novels. But allegory is a different and less attractive matter, as he says in this same Preface. In allegory "each image means something and is a term in the argument and nearly always for a moral or didactic purpose." [23] Each image means something. It is unfortunate that, attempting symbol and myth, Lawrence almost always arrived at allegory. But mindlessness is more difficult than one thinks; mindlessness and didactic purpose are hard to reconcile; and Lawrence proved to be better as educator than as symbolist.

Women in Love is a splendid example of the educational novel. It is a religious allegory like *Pilgrim's Progress,* which it resembles in everything except value, perhaps, and art. As Lawrence tells us in the Preface we have been discussing, he did not like Bunyan very much because Bunyan was an allegorist with a meaning. Lawrence could endure neither rivals nor predecessors, however, and he was unable to tolerate in others what he displayed himself. An accidental difference in doctrine and ethics may also have hidden from him and his readers what should have been plain. Bunyan and Lawrence are similar in class consciousness, obscurantism, and enthusiasm; and the characters and incidents of *Women in Love* show as clearly as these other similarities that Lawrence was the Bunyan of our day. *Pilgrim's Progress* is the story of Christian's conversion, in spite of the blandishments of false sectarians along the way, which he follows with the aid of Evangelist, a Baptist

[23] *Phoenix,* pp. 295–96.

minister. In *Women in Love* Ursula corresponds to Christian, Birkin to Evangelist, and most of the others to false sectarians. The plot concerns Ursula's conversion through many difficulties and backslidings to Lawrence's theory of the unconscious with the aid of Birkin, who corrects her errors and ministers to her wants. In the end she is saved by the living blood of Lawrence as Christian by the blood of Jesus. Along the way are false travelers who try to lure her from it. Hermione corresponds to Talkative, who, though having all the right answers, turns out to be a hypocrite. In spite of her pretense of mindlessness Birkin sees she is an intellectual. False-traveler Gerald strays from the path and falls down an Alp, as the false travelers of Bunyan perish in pits or mines. Mr. Wordly Wiseman reappears as the irreverent Bohemians who persecute Birkin with their sneers in the Vanity Fair of Bloomsbury. As a teacher Birkin uses the method of Evangelist and Greatheart: he teaches by examples. Greatheart draws spiritual lessons from the hen, the flowers, and other natural objects, Birkin from the domestic cat and the flowers. He tells Ursula about the meaning of stamen and pistil, at which she almost swoons, for they have "some strange, almost mystic-passionate attraction for her." As Bunyan's wicked characters are usually of the upper classes, the rich and the mighty, and his good characters of the lower, so Lawrence's Hermione and Gerald are rich, civilized, and irreligious, his Ursula, Birkin, and Loerke poor, low in rank, and spiritual. As Bunyan preached against intellect and learning, which keep the soul from salvation, so

Lawrence. This parallel across the centuries implies no influence, but it almost persuades one to accept Vico's notion that history repeats itself.

Lawrence as an educator made the novel his principal instrument, but he also had ideas about schools for the young. Education, he said, should be primarily religious in order to keep the innocence of children intact. Since mental knowledge is as fatal to the young as to the old, all schools except those devoted to handicrafts and primitive methods of fighting should be closed. By these exercises the dark, dynamic centers of the unconscious might prosper as the mind decayed. ("Bowels," said Bunyan, "becometh Pilgrims.") Annable, the gamekeeper of *The White Peacock,* practices what Lawrence preached. He is a graduate of Cambridge, but he has gone native, allowing his children to run wild in a state of nature.

In many ways Lawrence's diagnosis and his cure are foolish, but it would be unfair to dismiss them without asking how far they were justifiable and how they may be explained. It is true that many men of the eighteenth and nineteenth centuries had emphasized reason at the expense of emotion, and equally true that many had not. It is true that many men of the nineteenth century had been abused by the claims of materialistic science and that some of the troubles of our age may be traced to the machine. It is true that intellect is more or less out of place in love and political oratory and that the emotions are of value. Lawrence's complicated effort to proclaim the value of the emotions may have been of some use as a corrective to the dogmatic rationalism and science of the preceding period. But like many cures it was more excessive than the complaint. It was like curing gout with a bomb. Lawrence's cure, however foolish, may be explained by his nature and by that of our times.

As for Lawrence's nature, it was emotional but not without mind. Lawrence was right to insist in that bitter essay "Accumulated Mail" that when it came to intellect he was as well endowed as his critics.[24] There can be no doubt that he was an intellectual and that his attacks upon the mind are as mental as their object. It is also plain that, like Bunyan, he was even more naturally given to intellectual exposition than to allegory. His hero Birkin as usual reflects his creator's nature. This creature, who goes about rebuking intellect wherever it shows its head, is the most intellectual character of *Women in Love*. Gudrun is far from wrong when in a moment of wickedness she accuses him of being interested less in women than in his theories. Birkin and Lawrence were intellectual to the point of tedium, but their theories were so completely involved with and led by their emotions as to satisfy neither mind nor emotion. If Lawrence could have suppressed his intellect, the result might have been pleasing and lyrical. If he could have controlled his emotions, the result might have been art—or at least sense. But his intellect and his emotions remained more than normally confused. His quandary, more common in women than in men, partly explains the character of his campaign against the mind, which might more properly have taken the form, as it was the result, of a civil war.

[24] *Phoenix*, p. 805.

Lawrence's religious temper must also be considered. In the first chapter we noticed the growth of his enthusiasm, and in the present chapter we have seen that Lawrence preferred religion to science, that he longed for a return to "the old religious faculty" of intuition and wonder, and that upon this faculty, as remote as possible from the inductive method of science, he based his unverified conclusions. Dogma in itself was a cure for science. Mindlessness became a dogma of his religion. In the words of Ursula, Lawrence thought it "so *irreverent* to think that everything must be realized in the head." [25] To him mind seemed, unlike the bowels, to belong to the world of matter, and to the religious man matter and materialism are generally intolerable. Lawrence surveyed the age of materialism with disfavor, and his campaign against mind became a crusade.

The nature of the times partly justifies, as his enthusiastic temper partly explains, Lawrence's crusade, which was, however, only one of the most extreme of many. His predecessors and contemporaries, likewise confronted with the age of matter, had reacted and were reacting in a similar way. By the time of Lawrence the response of literary men to the age had fallen into a pattern or had become what historians call a tendency, a course which writers, like schools of fish, flights of angels, and other congregations of the deep, mysteriously follow. Though it owed much to his temper, Lawrence's crusade against matter and mind owed as much, if not more, to fashion.

A survey of the antimaterialistic tendency in recent

25 *Women in Love,* p. 160.

times [26] involves a consideration of its opposite. For convenience we may start with the publication of *The Origin of Species*. The controversy over this book brought before the public as nothing since Newton had done the idea of a mechanical and material universe. The sorrow of the pious swelled with the delight of advanced and liberal philosophers like John Morley, Annie Besant, and the husband of George Eliot, whose optimism, whose faith in progress and in reason found support in each development of science. Even the Philistines, after some doubts, accepted survival of the fittest as the corroboration of *laissez faire*. For many, determinism quietly took the place of predestination. As the ideas of determinism and materialism, the faith in reason, science, and progress, grew in the liberal and the Philistine mind, industry and the machine continued with increasing rapidity to change and disrupt society and to turn out hideous wallpaper. As it did so, the machine was hailed by most as the means and the hope of unending progress, but some could not abide it. Literature, which, like the cabbage, takes substance, shape, and flavor from its soil and time, reflected these hopes or fears.

Chief among the literary men who accepted science were the naturalists, Zola and his followers. In his essay *The Experimental Novel*, 1880, Zola proposed an art based on the new science, using for its realistic purpose the theory of strict determinism through natural forces. Heredity and environment, studied in detail and with

[26] For a survey of the antimaterialism and anti-intellectualism of the late eighteenth and early nineteenth centuries see Hoxie Neale Fairchild, *The Romantic Quest* (New York, Columbia University Press, 1931), especially Chapter VI, pp. 103–22.

aid of a notebook, would move human machines through the pages of the scientific novel. Passion, the closing of a door, the feeding of the cat, and all the trouble of the day were determined by nature and its laws. Now for the first time, enlightened and provided with a method by science, the novelist could see the causes and the meaning of what men and other animals do. Inspired by the experimental method and dazzled by Darwin, Zola produced his novels, each more frightful, each more uncompromising than the last. Inspired by Zola and dazzled by himself, George Moore wrote *A Mummer's Wife,* 1885, and the triumph of the disciple appeared to support the contentions of the master. It may be alleged against these literary scientists that they were not so scientific as they believed and that their faith in the possibilities of science was as premature as their attempt to apply the method of the laboratory was mistaken. But whatever their excess, it must be said of them, as of the scientists, that they prudently stopped short of the unknowable. Their excess, which is explained by the optimism of the time, was less than that of the popular poets who sang of progress and the machine. Kipling saw that natural selection and survival of the fittest meant progress from the ape to the imperial Englishman. He delighted in piston and connecting rod (which rhymes conveniently with God), he celebrated the engines as well as the guns of British ships, and he discovered romance in the arrival of the nine-fifteen. Henley, dashing over the roads in a 1901 Mercedes, offered his "Song of Speed" to her pipes and her cylinders. His faith in the material conquest of nature, in

a better and more mechanical world, and in his acquaintance with the purpose of God is similar, if we ignore
God, to that of Jules Verne, of the reader of *Popular
Science,* and of the creator of the comic strip in which
the young man goes about in a rocket. Hardy, however,
drew nothing but gloom from the mechanical universe.
He saw his human puppets "click-clack off its pread-
justed laws," he accepted with sorrow the blind indifference of nature, and the sound of his tears accompanied
the joyous shouts of Henley. Whether they laughed or
cried over it, these artists shared with the men of science
and with many ordinary men the idea of mechanism
and of life as an accident in matter. But these artists
were less numerous than their more sensitive or perhaps
more spiritual fellows, who rejected law, matter, and
the machine. Life, they thought, must—and indeed it
may—mean more than that.

Of these sensitive men, the aesthetes were among the
first. They observed the society and the hideous wallpaper created by the machine, and they fled from mechanical ugliness to refined sensations, pausing only to
recommend beauty and strangeness as the remedy for
what they saw in their backward glance. Tenderly and
without the assistance of machines they made ivory tow-
ers, domestic utensils, and love. Oscar Wilde, their apostle
to the world, who took upon himself the task of elevating the public taste by bringing blossoms to Piccadilly,
expressed with youthful exaggeration the sentiments of
his masters in his "Garden of Eros," 1881. Here the poet
deplored Natural Warfare and insensate Chance, the
iron roads and whirring wheels, the factories, the analy-

sis of the rainbow, and the other impediments to beauty
in this scientific age. He asked:

Shall I, the last Endymion, lose all hope
Because rude eyes peer at my mistress through a telescope!

And he replied:

Ah! there is something more in that bird's flight
Than could be tested in a crucible!—

Swinburne, Morris, Rossetti, and the Spirit of Beauty,
he hoped, would be influential enough to keep at least
that bird's flight out of the pot.

In France, at the same time, writers of the symbolist
school were in active rebellion against the materialism
and the externality of science and literature. They found
relief in a world of evocation and suggestion, in what
Verlaine called nuances and the vague. The two leading dramatists of this group show this more clearly than
some of the lyricists. The castle imagined by Villiers de
l'Isle-Adam symbolizes the contempt of the world felt by
Axel, the adept. The plays of Maeterlinck, with their
mysterious forests, their closed or open doors, and the
faint, tremulous beings on the doorsteps, suggest all that
is opposite to science, reason, and matter. Strindberg,
studying the occult in Paris, abandoned his earlier naturalism to dramatize states of soul. And even George
Moore, the disciple of Zola, betrayed his master and,
with the example of the symbolists and Pater before
him, turned to Biblical narrative and to the collection
of unintellectual poetry. These refugees of the eighties
and nineties were less articulate about the causes and
the end of their flight than William Butler Yeats, who,
although he imitated Maeterlinck and Villiers de l'Isle-

Adam in some of his early plays, had arrived at his spiritual and symbolist position long before he had heard of the French. His early work is parallel to, rather than part of, the symbolist movement, but it took its character from a similar hatred of abstraction and materialism. With the other theosophists he made his home in a world of spirits, magically summoned from the deep, from which A.E., though sharing his friend's dislike of the machine, also emerged at times, on a bicycle, to recommend cream separators to the peasantry.

To most of these spiritual, or all but spiritual, men the intellect appeared to be useless or harmful, science deplorable, and what they could not understand profound. These appearances, however, did not keep some of them from writing excellently. Nor did their similar convictions keep certain contemporary philosophers from philosophizing.

Nietzsche, in the steps of Schopenhauer, exalted will and power at the expense of intellect. Bergson left mathematics and physical science for a less mechanical way to reality, which, looking within, he found to be flow. Intuition was his instrument and the life-force his hope. Following first one, then the other of these philosophers, the intellectual Bernard Shaw combined their conclusions with Samuel Butler's hatred of machines and determinism and began in his turn to preach against science in favor of supermanly power and the life-force. His *Doctor's Dilemma*, 1906, exposed the nonsense of inoculation and bacteria, but this attack on science is as nothing compared with that in the Preface to *Back to Methuselah*, 1921, one of the most interesting documents of the recent revolt against materialism. Here he attacked the blind chance of Darwin and Huxley, saw starvation of the soul in the materialistic nihilism of the nineteenth century, labeled himself a "Vitalist philosopher," and proposed the religion of the life-force as a refuge from the nihilists. Shaw is more spiritual than his intelligence and the opinion of Yeats, who saw him as a smiling sewing-machine, suggest.

The spiritual nineties, surviving after their term in men like Shaw and Yeats, were followed by the materialistic Edwardian period. Wells pursued the nineteenth-century faith in science, reason, and material progress to a nineteenth-century Utopia, a cross between the Crystal Palace and the Five-Year Plan. Arnold Bennett, continuing the naturalism of Zola and Moore, wrote one of the best and least metaphysical novels of our time. Almost alone among his important contemporaries Bennett accepted and enjoyed the material world, which rewarded his devotion with a yacht. From the blight of this pedestrian and worldly period, the spirit began to revive shortly before the war, with the accession of George V. The literature which historians will call Georgian has been, with a few important exceptions, as inhospitable to matter and mind as that of the nineties.

Mr. Bennett and Mrs. Brown, addressed in 1924 to the spirits of Bloomsbury, now interests the historian. In this Georgian manifesto, Virginia Woolf rebuked her materialistic predecessors, Bennett, Wells, and Galsworthy, for elaborately pursuing and failing to catch Mrs. Brown or life itself. The Georgians, however, bored from within, she said, and surprised the soul in its den.

By soul, life, or Mrs. Brown, Mrs. Woolf meant not what a divine might suppose but the subjective, and by soulful the subjective approach. Henry James, dissatisfied with the externality of the naturalists, had invented his impressionism. Dissatisfied with the externality of the Edwardians, Virginia Woolf devised a fluid stream in which Mrs. Brown could float or disport herself, and the soul was freed from Mr. Bennett. Other Georgians found relief from materialism in the subjective technique, but Mrs. Woolf found more than the others. Life in her novels is flow, man a fish or a wave, and his only certainty a sense of immersion. Without, in the world of matter and machines, Big Ben strikes the alien hours as, within, the flow pursues its individual time. Intellect and abstraction are as alien as the clock to the current of life where the fish swim, pleasantly uncertain whether it is Monday or Tuesday and they male or female. Striding on his terrace with the problem of Q and R before him, Mr. Ramsay illustrates the limitations of the intellect. But Mrs. Ramsay, as limited intellectually as her husband is limited by intellect, sits suitably deliquescent in her chair. Life, said Mrs. Woolf in her essay "Modern Fiction," 1919, is not order imposed from without but a nebulous confusion, to which the novelist, discarding order and plunging softly within, must be true.

The novels of Mrs. Woolf, however, appear to be true to the philosophy of Bergson. She has never read him, she says, but one may know a philosopher one has never read if one has a sister-in-law who has written a book about him. Mrs. Woolf's concern with clocks, duration, and flux and her smiles at abstraction and science show not only the strength of fashion but that of family ties. Her novels also owe something to the Russian novelists, especially Dostoievsky, who enjoyed a vogue in Bloomsbury after 1912 because his works appeared to support the progress of the Georgians from external order to inner confusion. Freud and Jung also had their effect on her novels, as they had upon most English literature after 1910. Though men of science, these psychoanalysts revealed the unconscious and the libido, as dark, congenial mysteries to those already trying to discredit science or reason.

Adding its influence to that of Freud, Bergson, and the Russians, French symbolism, which resumed its interrupted course in England about 1912, revealed poetry to some poets, to others the charm of the irrational. The imagists, swooning at the fall of a fruit or over the color of a tile, found in Bergson, Hulme, and the lesser symbolists the way to girlish enthusiasm and to sensation. The rococo Miss Sitwell and her baroque brother engaged, according to her, in a battle against materialism. Herbert Read, the follower of Hulme, Bergson, and the psychoanalysts, combined flux, dogma, and enthusiasm with a taste for the solemn and the profound in his flight from reason and wit. He finally found his spiritual home in the dreams of the surrealists: deserted cities, herrings on the wall, and soft-boiled watches hanging from the trees. Except for Lawrence the surrealists are the outstanding rebels against the intellect. Freud, the symbolists, and the lunatic jests of Dada showed them the way to the unconscious, to instinct, and to insanity. Their aim is nonsense. They differ from Lawrence in that, of those who achieve nonsense, those who have tried to are better.

It is plain that others before, with, and after Lawrence shared his distrust of intellect and his discovery of the dark places of the soul, which Mrs. Woolf calls the only concern for moderns. It is plain that Lawrence is part of a general tendency and, what is more, its epitome. Others hated the world of mind or of matter; others proposed flow, sensation, vitalism, the unconscious, or the profound; but in Lawrence all these are united. For this reason he is of interest to his readers and of convenience to the historian, who may trace through him the pattern followed by the contemporary and his soul.

Lawrence had read, or was otherwise acquainted with, many of the writers within the pattern as well as the earlier writers of similar tendency such as Herakleitos and Rousseau.[27] During his formative period he read Schopenhauer, Nietzsche, and Butler's *Erewhon*.[28] He referred to Shaw's *Back to Methuselah* shortly after its appearance, and he may have read this important vitalist attack upon materialism.[29] In 1913 he read a book by Bergson, probably *Creative Evolution,* if we may judge by Lawrence's many references to the *élan vital*.[30] His works seem to depend almost as much as those of Mrs. Woolf on a first- or secondhand acquaintance with Bergson's theories.[31] But Lawrence spoke as harshly about

---

[27] *Letters,* p. 716; *Movements in European History,* p. 269; *Phoenix,* p. 751; *Porcupine,* p. 229; *Studies in Classic American Literature,* p. 36.

[28] E. T., *D. H. Lawrence, a Personal Record,* pp. 101–33.

[29] *Fantasia,* p. 103.

[30] *Letters,* p. 119; *Fantasia,* p. 15; *Phoenix,* p. 647.

[31] Many passages in *Psychoanalysis* on concepts, abstractions, direct expression of flux, etc., sound like Bergson. Cf. "Life is not a question

Bergson and Shaw as he did about materialists like Joyce,
Bennett, Strachey, and Wells. We have already noticed
that Lawrence commonly attacked books he found useful. We must consider, however, that consistency or intellectual honesty would have been illogical in one who
repudiated logic and unnatural in one so confused. With
similar expressions of distaste and equal profit, he read
Jung,[32] whose libido is another version of the life-force,
and probably Freud; he read Dostoievsky at the height
of the vogue and in an unguarded moment confessed
that the Russians had meant much to him; [33] he read
Verlaine, Maeterlinck, and other symbolists.[34] But more
important than books was the air of Bloomsbury, in
which he expanded in company with the fashionable.
He knew Richard Aldington and H. D., Edward Garnett
and Middleton Murry—both of whom were authorities
on Dostoievsky—and Koteliansky, who knew Virginia
Woolf as well as the Russians. The pattern had been
traced, and Lawrence naturally followed it in his response to circumstances and times like those which had
traced it. If his response to the confusion of the times
appears completer and more extravagant than fashion
required, the reason may be found in his private sorrows
and in his own confusion.

---

of points, but a question of flow." *Assorted Articles,* p. 50. Lawrence's
antipathy to the clock in *The Plumed Serpent,* like Woolf's Big Ben,
seems to be a dramatization of Bergson's ideas about mechanical or
clock time vs. duration.

[32] *Fantasia,* p. 15: here he mentions Jung's libido or life-force together
with the *élan vital.* Cf. *Apocalypse,* p. 144; *Letters,* p. 458.

[33] *Letters,* pp. 198, 238, 313, 383, and *passim; Phoenix,* p. 283.

[34] E. T., *Personal Record; Letters,* p. 196.

CHAPTER THREE

ANIMAL, VEGETABLE, OR
MINERAL LOVE

MINDLESSNESS pleased and confused Lawrence, but deeper pleasure and profounder confusion were to be had, he discovered, from what he called sometimes relationship, sometimes contact, polarity, or love. In these or this, as in the other elements of his religion, the hopeful nominalist found a cure for what ailed him and the world.

The chaos of the world and man's spiritual isolation may be traced to several causes, none greater, perhaps, than the individualism of Protestants and of capitalists. Lawrence was not a capitalist, but he had been, and in a sense still was, a Protestant. His announcement that he was an individualist was neither unnatural nor misleading. In his *Movements in European History* he says, with some exaggeration, that Luther led the individual to believe as the soul moved him, to act as the heart desired in "beautiful, flexible freedom." [1] Without his Protestant training, however, Lawrence probably would have shared the all but universal notion; for as the older traditions decline, individualism, a cause of their decline, is almost the only substantial tradition left. To have remained immune from it would have required a stronger and a less fashionable mind than his. But like

[1] Pages 239, 249.

many other men of his time, he lamented the effects of the destructive tradition he had chosen. To cure these effects he proposed his theory of relationship, which, since it was shared by nobody else, was similar to the cause of what it was designed to cure. His confusion may be explained by the historian or the psychologist, who considers the state of the times or of Lawrence; it might be condemned by the Bishop of Rome or applauded by the homeopath; but it could not remedy confusion.

Sometimes Lawrence seems to have felt the difficulty of maintaining a theory of individualism along with one of relationship, but even in theory his individualism sometimes remained unimpaired by his individualistic cure for individualism. His works are filled with statements or ejaculations on the importance of the particular soul, whose perfection is the goal of life and whose singleness would suffer from merging with a greater thing.[2] On the other hand his works are filled with statements of the need of contact or union with another or greater thing, often at the cost of identity.[3] In *Apocalypse,* for example, he rejects individuality in favor of oneness with all.[4] At times he wavered between preserving identity and merging with the whole, preferring, in the same essay, now one now the other.[5] At other times, however, he tried to reconcile relationship with individuality by making the former a necessary condition for the attainment of the latter.

[2] For example, *Psychoanalysis*, p. 106; *Phoenix,* pp. 600, 635, 638, 703–5, 714, 740; *Fantasia*, pp. 20, 25–26.

[3] *Phoenix,* pp. 188, 669, 694, 761; *Letters,* pp. 265–66.

[4] *Apocalypse,* pp. 199–200.

[5] "Education of the People," *Phoenix:* cf. p. 615 with pp. 634–38.

A natural effect of individualism, whether simple, confused, or reconciled, is the sense of isolation. The growth of Lawrence's singularity was accompanied by his complaints of social and spiritual loneliness. Lawrence said to a friend who proposed a group-movement:

I should love to be connected with something, with some few people, in something. As far as anything *matters,* I have always been very much alone, and regretted it. But I can't belong to clubs, or societies. . . . So if there is, with you, an activity I *can* belong to, I shall thank my stars. . . . I shall be very glad to abandon my rather meaningless isolation, and join in with some few other men, if I can.[6]

To another correspondent he complained of the frustration of his "primeval societal instinct" and, seeing for a moment the cause, exclaimed, "I am weary of my own individuality." [7] He represented his nature and his plight in those of Somers, the hero of *Kangaroo,* who is as remarkable for his unwillingness and inability to make friends as he is loud in his complaints of friendlessness. "He was the most forlorn and isolated creature in the world." With good reason his wife calls him a Phoenix, and if the loneliness rather than the renewal of that fowl is considered, Lawrence had reason as good for his choice of symbol. The war and the disorder of society intensify the isolation which nature and theory have imposed upon Somers. He feels that he has been torn loose from England, Europe, tradition, and his fellow men. " 'Where is my Rock of Ages?' " this individualist asks, and finding it at last to lie heavy within himself he returns for refuge, with heavier heart, to his individualism, which now

[6] *Letters,* p. 667; cf. *Assorted Articles,* pp. 152–53.
[7] *Letters,* p. 685; cf. *Phoenix,* pp. 377 ff.

seems less Rock than plank. "He was loose like a single timber of some wrecked ship, drifting over the face of the earth." That a timber should drift over the face of the earth is no more unnatural than the situation of Mr. Somers.[8]

Relationship between or among men and union in a common belief,[9] remedies which Lawrence advocated for the distemper of the singular way, were singular but not unparalleled; nor was he alone in his complaint or diagnosis. T. S. Eliot also felt the pains of isolation; and, as London Bridge was falling down, he heard the collapse of individualistic society and saw the need of connection with some solid thing. There were others, too, wandering alone among the fragments, testing the solidity of this or that. The Waste Land became crowded with spiritual orphans in search of rich relations. Eliot found his in the creed of the Anglo-Catholics, Lawrence his in a more private belief. Though Lawrence's relationship and Eliot's Canterbury deadened the sense of isolation which had inspired them, these religious cures for individualism, as I shall show in a later chapter, were among its least pleasing effects. Lawrence and Eliot grasped at last straws.

What Lawrence called relationship seemed to him, at such times as he reconciled it with individuality, to be the way of restoring the warm flow of sympathy between men, women, animals, plants, and minerals, of uniting men in a common belief, and of perfecting the individual. Real individuality, he held, comes only from rela-

[8] *Kangaroo,* pp. 192, 195, 291, 314; cf. pp. 112–15, 250, 255, 281, 315, 317.

[9] *Letters,* p. 688; *Assorted Articles,* p. 154; *Women in Love,* pp. 63–64.

tionship.[10] During and immediately after the war, Lawrence preferred to call relationship polarity, perhaps
because under that name the idea seemed less desperate.

His first systematic accounts of polarity appeared in
Psychoanalysis and the Unconscious, 1921, and *Fantasia
of the Unconscious,* of the next year, both written in
1921 after he had broken off relations with England and
attempted fresh ones first with Italy, then with Germany.
Polarity occurs below the neck in the unconscious; so
Lawrence knew a great deal about it. As far as it concerns
men and women, this tender and unknowable process
involves several centers and circuits. The unconscious,
which, as we have already seen, has four principal centers,
is divided by the diaphragm into two levels, a lower dark-
dynamic level and an upper objective-dynamic level. On
the lower are the centers of the solar plexus and of the
lumbar ganglion; on the upper, the cardiac plexus and
the thoracic ganglion. Of the upper level Lawrence knew
everything save for one thing: "We do not know," he
said, "how the nipples of the breast are as fountains leap-
ing into the universe, or as little lamps irradiating the
contiguous world, to the soul in quest." [11] But no matter.
He knew that each of the levels and centers or poles is
charged with attractive or repulsive energy, that each is
either positive or negative. The upper level is negative
with respect to the lower, and with respect to the upper
the lower is positive; within the lower the solar plexus is
positive, the lumbar ganglion negative; in both planes
the front poles are relatively positive, the aft negative.

[10] *Psychoanalysis,* p. 68; *Phoenix,* pp. 188, 190; *Porcupine,* p. 162;
Assorted Articles, pp. 102–4.
[11] *Psychoanalysis,* p. 83.

Between the poles on each plane and between the planes there flows, as between the poles of a magnet or a battery, a flow of "lovely polarized vitalism." This circuit among the four poles of the unconscious is fourfold polarity. But when the circuit is also, as it should be, with the four poles of another unconscious, the polarity is eightfold. With the additional poles which Lawrence discovered later, the hypogastric, the sacral, and the cervical, the circuit within the individual unconscious and with another unconscious becomes more formidable; but we may postpone the thought of it. Roughly speaking, for relationship with another and for the establishment of individuality, perfect eightfold positive and negative polarity is enough. The attractive, positive circuit unites man with others, but union alone is imperfect. The repulsive energy of the negative poles must also establish individual identity. In a word, eightfold, positive and negative, dynamic, vitalistic, unconscious, balanced polarity is love.

Love is not a distraction but a way of worship, a process of soul, a sacrament through which the individual is saved or "born again." [12] Benjamin Franklin's advice to "use venery" for convenience, health, and offspring was too prudent and reasonable for a man so religious as Lawrence. Rejecting Franklin and materialism with horror, Lawrence rescued venery from "use" and claimed it for religion as "An offering-up of yourself to the very great gods, the dark ones, and nothing else." [13] He could never regard the idea of two and one, which love naturally im-

[12] *Letters*, p. 265; *Tales*, p. 891; *Aaron's Rod*, p. 195.
[13] *Classic American Literature*, pp. 20, 26.

plies, without an emotion too deep for articulate expression: "The duality goes so far and is so profound. And the polarity!" [14] The profound duality of love seemed one of flesh and spirit, the flesh being the province of the level below the diaphragm, the spirit of that above, or sometimes vice versa. Out of the consummation of flesh and spirit or out of the polarity of levels and centers is created the Holy Ghost, and flesh becomes the Word. The spark arising from the balance of two individuals is also the Holy Ghost.[15]

At times love seemed to Lawrence not the way of worship but the way or approach to worship. At these times, as always, religious purpose, "the essentially religious or creative motive," remained his goal, but it was no longer identical with love. Love, now subordinate to purpose, became a preprophetical necessity. After polarity and rebirth, man leaves his bed to go out to make the world anew. In *Psychoanalysis and the Unconscious* polarity is the resurrection and the life; in *Fantasia* polarity, though not divorced from the religious motive, is secondary to it. But this was a matter of emphasis and a distinction not generally observed.[16]

Lawrence first used the verb polarize in 1914 in a short story "Daughters of the Vicar" and the noun polarity in 1915 in a letter to Lady Cynthia Asquith [17] on the articles he was then writing for *The Signature* and *The English Review*. These effusions, published between 1915 and 1918—"The Crown," "The Reality of Peace," "Love,"

[14] *Psychoanalysis*, p. 94.
[15] *Letters*, pp. 96–97, 100, 265, 361, 625–26; *Porcupine*, pp. 17, 23–27, 28, 94, 97, 141; *Fantasia*, pp. 40–41, 99; *Phoenix*, pp. 528, 535.
[16] *Fantasia*, pp. 14, 97–99, 100, 111. [17] *Tales*, p. 84; *Letters*, p. 292.

and "Life"—in which the word polarity is used less frequently than it was later on, are his first on relationship. Under the imagery of lions, lambs, and even unicorns he discusses duality and the balance of opposites by attraction and repulsion in a new equilibrium of two in one, yet one and one. In this partnership of lion and lamb he found the only likable absolute in a relative world. Positive and negative polarity, circuits, and the solar plexus, the machinery behind the unnatural marriage of mutton with carnivore, are described in "The Education of the People," a long essay of about the year 1920, a study for *Psychoanalysis* and *Fantasia*.[18]

The question, which I shall not answer fully now, of where Lawrence got the word polarity and the idea behind it is a difficult one, since Lawrence's philosophy is a synthesis of odds and ends from his reading and experience, interpreted to suit his needs. As E. T. remarks, Lawrence's interest in the works he read was never academic and what he found in his reading never without application to his desires. For the present it will be enough to suggest a few of the obvious sources for his idea of relationship. The word polarity was in common use throughout the nineteenth century, by scientists who used it with reference to magnetism, electricity, and light and by literary men who used it in the more general senses of force, of relationship between organisms, or of opposites. Schelling, whose strange philosophy has much in

[18] See also the early versions of his essays on American literature as published in *The English Review*, 1918–19, and the references to positive and negative infinites in *Twilight in Italy*, pp. 50, 81. In the latter volume, "The Lemon Gardens" appears to be a preliminary study for "The Crown."

common with that of Lawrence, frequently used the term in his intuitive pursuit of the life-force through the mysteries of attraction and repulsion, organic and inorganic, static and dynamic. As far as I know there is no evidence that Lawrence read Schelling, but he did read, with pleasure, the essays of Emerson, who was equally fond of the word polarity. In his wide reading in nineteenth-century science and philosophy Lawrence had opportunity to find the word used in every sense he could desire.

The idea of relationship or balance is implied in many uses of the word polarity, but Lawrence seems to have had other sources for that idea. In Hegel, whom he read and admired, Lawrence could have found the idea of changing duality and the confusion of opposites out of which something new develops. Though Hegel may have been of some use, the early Greeks, who fascinated Lawrence, appear to have been of more, as one of his later essays makes clear. The Greeks, he said, made equilibrium their goal as he does, but what they called equilibrium he calls relationship.[19] It was simple for a passionate eclectic to apply the word polarity to Greek or Hegelian duality and, with the help of the theories of the life-force and the unconscious and of a theory of the bodily centers, which I shall discuss in a later chapter, to apply the result to his experience.

From his relationships with his mother, with the girl known as Miriam or E. T., with the schoolmistress at Croydon, with Frieda, and later with his disciples, he discovered a way of salvation in love, together with much about good and bad polarities which found place in his

[19] *Porcupine,* pp. 134–35, 137.

system and, assisted by his fancy, also helped him to interpret his experience before and after he had had it. His connection with Miriam was injured, he felt, by her mind, and his interest in other women was impaired by their wills. In his theory, mind and will became fatal to relationship, though Schopenhauer [20] and Nietzsche, whom he otherwise liked, had spoken well of the latter faculty. Lawrence found Frieda attractive, but their relationship was not without an element of the repulsive. Witnesses have reported in their memoirs the battles between these lovers, around whose heads cups, saucers, and other domestic objects not infrequently flew. It is said that Lawrence broke cups with a poker, that Frieda broke plates over his head. [21] They loved each other very much. From his experience with his wife Lawrence may have learned the need of negative as well as positive polarity. From his mother he found the effect of imperfect relationship between husband and wife, such as that between his father and mother, to be an improper relationship between mother and son. He devoted much of *Fantasia* and several other essays to the Oedipus complex and to its prevention by dynamic eightfold polarity for the parents, by spanking for the child. [22]

Experience with willful women, who could not keep

[20] In 1908 Lawrence was impressed with Schopenhauer's essay "The Metaphysics of Love," in *Essays*, translated by Mrs. Rudolph Dircks (Walter Scott, 1903): see E. Delavenay, *"Sur un exemplaire de Schopenhauer annoté par D. H. Lawrence,"* *Revue Anglo-Américaine*, treizième année (February, 1936), pp. 234–38.

[21] Cf. the battles between Somers and Harriet in *Kangaroo*, pp. 197, 266, and the quarrels described by Knud Merrild.

[22] For example, *Fantasia*, pp. 43–44, 106–11, 117, 126; *Phoenix*, pp. 621, 632, 640; *Letters*, p. 458. "The Lovely Lady" in the story of that name is an Oedipus vampire.

from pursuing, dominating, or mothering him, seems to
have led Lawrence to improve his theory of balance. Balance remained balance, but equal circuits no longer
meant equal poles. The early image of lion and lamb was
a fortunate one; for the lion is not equal to the lamb with
whom he condescends to lie down. Let man be lion,
woman lamb. By becoming pursuer, master, creature of
will and idea, the feminine lamb had become feminist
lion, and the natural inequality of balance was reversed.
To correct the balance lion must be lion again, lamb
lamb. Superior man must create, inferior woman must
renew him, yielding to male power, pursuit, and leadership; for in man's will is woman's peace, not to mention
man's. During the pursuits of the day, under the eye of
hostesses and disciples, after the crash and tinkle of plates,
Lawrence may have found consolation in his improvements to the theory of balance.[23]

Before Lawrence redressed the balance, indeed before
he developed the idea of eightfold polarity and elevated
it to a theory of salvation, he had explored in his fiction
the possibilities of love. The stories written before he
met his wife differ from the later ones in being based, in
spite of certain pardonable fancies, upon observation of
the actual. For this reason most of these early stories deal
with imperfect love.

Sons and Lovers, 1913, deals with the relationships between the hero, his mother, and his beloved. The improper and defective connections among these three are
too well known to require comment, but the connections

[23] *Fantasia,* pp. 42, 76, 87–88, 88–89, 90, 92–93, 98, 99, 171, 173, 174;
Porcupine, pp. 153, 154, 171–75, 218; *Phoenix,* p. 196; *Letters,* pp. 458,
688.

studied in *The White Peacock,* 1911, are as unfortunate, less familiar, and no less diverting. Lettie, who is loved by Leslie, the civilized mine-owner, and by George, a milkman, sensibly marries the mine-owner. But denied perfect love, she dominates her husband and finds fulfillment through her children. George, also denied love in his marriage to a person of inferior quality, turns for satisfaction to socialism, drink, and horses. His wife is annoyed by this concern with the irrelevant and finds relief in her children. If this story of two defective marriages had been written later, it would have illustrated infractions of the law of polarity and their consequences. As it stands, it shows Lawrence's observation of his parents. Even without the aid of theory it is tragical—all but Greek—tracing as it does the fall of George from the estate of milkman to that of drunkard. In *The Trespasser,* 1912, Lawrence tells the story of Siegmund, a perfect Wagnerite,[24] who is married to an unfortunate woman. Leaving her to fret with her children, he spends a week end at the beach with Helena, another Wagnerite, who proves, however, to be otherwise incompetent; so he goes home and commits suicide. Unlike these tragedies, "Love among the Haystacks," a short story of 1912, is a pastoral fantasy in which two haymakers find suitable mates. One of the haymakers knows a Polish governess with whom, as he might have said ten years later, he wishes to be polarized; the other finds a woman who would do. The story ends with the fulfillment of the hay-

[24] The characters in this novel continually refer to Wagner, whom Lawrence appears to have adored as much as he detested eighteenth-century composers. Lawrence had no understanding of music.

makers, one at the top of the haystack, the other at the bottom.

Experience with Frieda, rationalized to fit the developing philosophy of which it was in part a source, made Lawrence's later novels and stories illustrations of the theory of love rather than aesthetic rearrangements of the actual. In the Foreword to *Fantasia* Lawrence claimed, however, that his novels depended upon experience, not upon his philosophy, which was deduced from the novels. It is true that his novels sometimes preceded systematic expressions of the philosophy such as *Psychoanalysis and the Unconscious;* but the novels and the systematic expressions of the philosophy alike were based upon the philosophy. As Lawrence admitted in *Fantasia:* ". . . art is utterly dependent on philosophy: or if you prefer it, on a metaphysic." The trouble with modern art, he continued, is that our age is without a belief or a metaphysic upon which the art may be founded.[25]

The belief upon which his extraordinary art was founded is stated in his essays on the novel. "The business of art," he said, "is to reveal the relation between man and his circumambient universe at the living moment." Of the arts, the novel is truest to flowing relationships between men, women, and all things and is the best aid to relatedness. It is the moralist's as well as the metaphysician's tool. "If a novel reveals true and vivid relationships, it is a moral work. . . . If the novelist *honours* the relationship in itself, it will be a great novel." [26]

Of Lawrence's great novels *The Rainbow,* 1915, is the

[25] *Fantasia,* pp. 10–11.   [26] *Phoenix,* pp. 525, 527–32, 534–35.

first in the order of time. This work consists of three case histories illustrating complete and incomplete polarity. The horrified public was unready for the new morality of relatedness and was without understanding of value, but Lawrence, who wrote because he wanted folk to alter,[27] continued his moral illustration of a metaphysic in *Women in Love,* 1920, written in 1916. In this, his profoundest study of polarity between men and women and men and men,[28] Lawrence provided several more case histories. Those of Gudrun and Gerald, of Birkin and Hermione, and of Birkin and Gerald show how will, mind, desire to dominate, and want of dark sensuality prevent eightfold dynamic relationship. That of Gudrun and Loerke is correct; that of Birkin and Ursula perfect. Ursula has what is needed, and Birkin has the proper theory of the "mystic" balance of two individuals, "like two poles of one force." " 'There is only the pure duality of polarisation . . .' " Birkin informs Ursula. " 'What I want is a strange conjunction with you . . . not meeting and mingling . . . but an equilibrium, a pure balance of two single beings:—as the stars balance each other.' " [29] By sermon and example he at last converts her from her desire for willful domination, merging, and intimacy to Lawrence's theory of love. Before this final happiness, in her simple way Ursula had thought love love.

By the time of *Aaron's Rod,* 1922, balance had been revised to mean male leadership. Aaron flees from his willful, dominating wife to seek the restoration of his

[27] *Letters,* p. 120.   [28] Cf. *Kangaroo,* pp. 265–69 and *passim.*
[29] *Women in Love,* pp. 165–68, 172–73, 227–28.

individuality in solitude and to await a new relationship, preached by Lilly, to whom he is strangely drawn as Birkin had been to Gerald, in which women must submit to male power and superiority.[30] When he is not urging Harriet to submit reverently to him, Somers of *Kangaroo*, 1923, is rejecting the advances of the Jew called Kangaroo, who pursues him with soft cries and tender embraces. The trouble with accepting the love of Kangaroo is not that he is a man or too portly but that he wants to dominate Somers as Somers wants to dominate Harriet. Besides, Kangaroo has the wrong theory of love.[31] He is too mental, chummy, and willful about it to be attractive.[32] *The Plumed Serpent*, 1926, continues the theme of unbalanced balance. In Cipriano, Kate finds her master; and her joy, far above that of ordinary love, is in mindless, impersonal, unequal yet somehow balanced communion with the boss.[33]

This manly notion of woman's place was also celebrated in short story and novelette, in "The Fox" and "The Captain's Doll," for example, or *St. Mawr,* all published between 1923 and 1925. The heroine of the last of these escapes from bad polarity and longs, while possessing her soul in private, for a man bigger, deeper, and more mysterious than she. Many other stories, like this one and like "The Ladybird," 1923, have the theme of women or men fleeing the unpolarized home to find or

[30] *Aaron's Rod,* pp. 185–96, 285–88, 346.
[31] When Somers condemns love in this novel, he is merely condemning love in the usual sense, not Lawrence's theory of love. Lawrence uses the word love in two senses throughout his work: (1) ordinary, (2) sublime or his own variety.
[32] *Kangaroo,* pp. 146–51, 233–35.
[33] *The Plumed Serpent,* pp. 331 ff., 453, 456.

to seek better contacts elsewhere or, remaining at home, to find love with a guest. "The Princess," 1925, holds up to scorn a woman who, even in the arms of a Mexican, is found wanting. These polar explorations, though exhausting more than their possibilities, seem trivial compared with *Lady Chatterley's Lover*, 1928.

The premise of this final dissertation, which seemed so tender and frail to its author that he shrank from having it profaned by typist's eye,[34] is that Lady C. is out of touch with everyone and everything. "Out of her disconnection, a restlessness was taking possession of her like madness." [35] What should she do to be saved? She goes for a walk in the woods. There Mellors, the gamekeeper, although his favorite word is "Nay," abandons his temporary isolation at the sight of the lady and restores her to connection with all things by impersonal sensuality. " 'Nay, nay,' " he exclaims. "And suddenly he held her fast against his breast again, with the old connecting passion." [36] Meanwhile, as polarity restores their souls in the woodland lodge, "the dog sighed with discomfort on the mat." [37]

As Mellors in saving Lady C., as Birkin in saving Ursula and in trying to save Gerald, so Lawrence in writing his novels of polarity was minding his business; for, as he said, the job of a saviour is to establish new relationships.[38] However interesting to the novelist or appealing to the susceptible saviour, the new relationships to be established by saviour or novelist are not merely those between man and woman or man and man. This kind of

---

[34] *Letters*, pp. 683, 708, 710.   [35] *Lady Chatterley*, pp. 14, 18–19, 20.
[36] *Ibid.*, p. 139.   [37] *Ibid.*, p. 246.   [38] *Porcupine*, pp. 228–29, 238.

love is but an approach to man's further relationship with the living universe, with sun, moon, earth, trees, flowers, and all the beasts of house or field. Through creatures and stars, holding them in dynamic equilibrium, flow circuits of vital attraction and repulsion. Eightfold polarity with another man or woman is necessary and convenient, but the final love, by which the individual is saved and renewed, is far more splendid: a mineral, animal, vegetable, many-fold polarity. "This is how I 'save my soul' by accomplishing a pure relationship between me and another person, me and other people . . . me and the animals, me and the trees or flowers, me and the earth, me and the skies and sun and stars, me and the moon: an infinity of pure relations, big and little, like the stars of the sky . . ." [39]

These loves beyond love suggest the aid of the nineteenth-century pantheists, vitalists, and transcendentalists, whose flights, compelled by the age which cut the pattern of their wings, suggested no less giddy flights to others less qualified to soar. Without doubt Lawrence's transcendental reading increased his altitude, but his love was too high, deep, and fierce to be so simply explained. Whitman, Emerson, and Thoreau, for example, can be accounted no more than indirectly responsible for Lawrence's highest love, that of the sun and moon, or for his deepest, that of the earth's dark core. The sun, he said, is the positive pole of the cosmic circuit. When his solar plexus was polarized with the sun, when he was "with the sun as a woman is with child," he felt less

[39] *Phoenix*, p. 528; cf. pp. 31, 202, and also *Porcupine*, pp. 140, 161, 184–87, 210–15, 223; *Fantasia*, p. 119; *Psychoanalysis*, pp. 52, 114; *Letters*, p. 688.

alone. To share the life he felt filled with at such moments, he said, man must know that

his greatest and final relation is with the sun, the sun of suns: and with the night, which is moon and dark and stars. In the last great connections, he lifts his body speechless to the sun. . . . Yes the actual sun! That which blazes in the day! Which scientists call a sphere of blazing gas—what a lot of human gas there is . . . and which the Greeks call Helios! The sun, I tell you, is alive. . . . it is the Holy Ghost in full raiment, shaking and walking. . . . And when I can turn my body to the sun, and say: "Sun! Sun!" and we meet—then I am come finally into my own.[40]

As the living sun is a positive pole for the well-connected man, the living earth and the moon are negative poles. Of the earth Lawrence had much to say. The "sulphureous" exhalations and the beautiful electricity of Mount Etna, for example, affected him profoundly: "Nay, sometimes, verily, one can feel a new current of her demon magnetism seize one's living tissue and change the peaceful life of one's active cells. She makes a storm in the living plasm and a new adjustment. And sometimes it is like a madness." [41] In Sardinia his feet thrilled in contact with the living granite of the earth. It was here also that he liked to walk "across the frozen cow-droppings: and," he added, "it is all so familiar to my *feet,* my very feet in contact . . ." [42] Of the moon he had less to say: "I can hardly talk about it," he said, "it goes so deep into one's bowels and makes one a little sick." [43] Lawrence's vital-

[40] *Porcupine,* p. 236; cf. pp. 184, 211, 214, and also *Fantasia,* pp. 138–48, 161.

[41] *Sea and Sardinia,* pp. 13, 15.   [42] *Ibid.,* p. 150.

[43] *Letters,* p. 455; cf. *Kangaroo,* p. 382: Somers gets in touch with the moon, feeling the "call and the answer, without intermediary." Cf. *ibid.,* pp. 170–71, on his feeling of contact with the sea.

istic astronomy affected I. A. Richards in the same way the moon had affected Lawrence.[44] Richards is a materialist, however, to whom earth, moon, and sun, the living objects of Lawrence's devotion, seem but mineral or gaseous.

Such mineral conclusions are far from the mindless mind of the heroine of Lawrence's story "Sun." This lady abandons her unsatisfactory husband, a business man of East 47th Street, for sun-bathing on the Mediterranean shore.

It was not just taking sunbaths. It was much more than that. Something deep inside her unfolded and relaxed, and she was given. By some mysterious power inside her, deeper than her own consciousness and will, she was put into connection with the sun, and the stream flowed of itself, from her womb . . . this dark flow from her deep body to the sun.[45]

Her polarity with the sun, the first relationship she has known, prepares her for a further polarity with a peasant, whose connections with all things have filled him with vital heat. The woman of "The Woman Who Rode Away" rides away from her husband to find consummation with the sun in becoming its victim. The heroes of *The Plumed Serpent* enjoy contacts with sun, moon, stars, and earth. But polarity with the sun or with plants and four-footed animals is not as common in Lawrence's novels as in his essays. It is perhaps because his essays are less familiar to the public that his name is associated almost exclusively, almost as if Lawrence were its discoverer, with love in the usual sense, though in this sense it had been known and, indeed, practiced before

[44] *Science and Poetry,* p. 91. [45] *Tales,* p. 746.

he celebrated it. An awareness of the limitations of the public, who expect a novel to deal with men and women, may have kept Lawrence from emphasis, except in his essays and in a few stories, upon other loves. His artistic sense may also have restrained him; for a novel dealing with the connection between a gamekeeper and broccoli, though as profound as one dealing with a gamekeeper and a lady, is less dramatical.

Of vegetable love, which had been mentioned by Andrew Marvell and known to Erasmus Darwin, Lawrence said something in *Fantasia,* more in later essays. Seated among the trees of the Black Forest, he felt connected, announced that trees have souls but no minds, and found his own soul to have been fed by the connection. Seated before a pine tree in New Mexico, some years later, he felt the tree vibrating into his soul, connecting him vitally, mystically with the earth and sky powers.[46] He loved the trees, but he did not neglect the smaller vegetables. His essays on the flowers show a long mastery of the subject.[47] Indeed, E. T. says that Lawrence when but a lad had subscribed to a nature-lovers' magazine. While none of the novels or stories of his later years is devoted to the love of trees or flowers, few are without some trace of it. *The White Peacock* is filled with love of green stuff. The strange creature who tells this story almost swoons with delight as he lies among, or eats, the flowers. As he loiters in the wilds of Australia, the poetical hero of *Kangaroo* lets "himself feel all sorts of things about the

[46] *Fantasia,* pp. 37–39; *Phoenix,* pp. 24–31; *Porcupine,* pp. 232–33.
[47] *Porcupine,* pp. 211–15, 231; *Phoenix,* pp. 45, 60–64; *Kangaroo,* pp. 396–99; *Twilight in Italy, passim.*

bush." [48] The heroine of "Sun" lies "balancing a lemon flower in her navel, laughing to herself." [49] The heroine of *St. Mawr* is lost in admiration of all that is natural and in the end finds polarity not with man but with mountains, flowers, and trees. "But beyond the pine-trees, ah, there beyond, there was beauty for the spirit to soar in." [50] Less devoted to the Beyond but as much concerned with blossoms, the gamekeeper decorates Lady Chatterley with forget-me-nots, oak sprays, bluebells, campions, and woodruff until she looks like an old-fashioned garden and he the gardener. Notwithstanding the thoroughness of this Voltairian cultivation, a purer example of vegetable love is to be found in *Women in Love*. In this novel, Hermione despairing, as a mental person might, of polarity finds her only possible consummation in violence. With a lapis lazuli paperweight she biffs Birkin on the head. Therefore, he removes his clothing and sits down among the primroses, curing by his contact with petal, leaf, and stem his unnatural contact with the paperweight. Then, finding primroses too soft, he rolls in the pine needles, which, though as stimulating as woman, seem far less dangerous. "This was his place, his marriage place."

. . . this was good, this was all very good, very satisfying. Nothing else would do . . . except this coolness and subtlety of vegetation traveling into one's blood. How fortunate he was, that there was this lovely, subtle, responsive vegetation, waiting for him, as he waited for it; how fulfilled he was, how happy! . . . He could love the vegetation and be quite happy and unquestioned, by himself.[51]

---

[48] *Kangaroo*, pp. 8–9.   [49] *Tales*, p. 745.   [50] *Ibid.*, p. 677.
[51] *Women in Love*, pp. 120–21, 122.

For the time he appears to have kept his back to nature.

Rousseau and Wordsworth, as well as Percy Shelley and Reginald Bunthorne, are suggested by the conduct of Birkin and the fancies of Lawrence. Such resemblances are not to be wondered at; for Lawrence is plainly in their tradition of nature worship. Wordsworth sat on the cold grey stone and, succumbing to one impulse from the vernal wood, let Nature be his teacher. The transcendental fleshly Bunthorne, at such times as he was free from his lady disciples, lay upon the daisies, content with his attachment à la Plato for a bashful young potato. Concerning Bunthorne, who differs from Lawrence in having been a sham, Lawrence had nothing to say, though he was familiar with the Gilbert and Sullivan operas. He knew, but rarely spoke well of, the work of Rousseau. He adored Shelley, whom he considered "a million thousand times more beautiful than Milton." [52] And, according to E. T., he read Wordsworth with almost equal passion. He admitted that Wordsworth, Rousseau, and Shelley had established a new connection between man and the universe; but he was at some pains in his New Mexican essays to distinguish himself from Wordsworth, whose connection with the universe seemed incorrect in some particulars. In the essay ". . . . Love Was Once a Little Boy," where he parodied Wordsworth's verses on the primrose, Lawrence objected that the poet was too anthropomorphic, too eager to merge himself with the flower and too intent upon the Oversoul. Lawrence was not always immune from the idea of the Oversoul or of merging, but here he preferred to

[52] *Letters,* p. 166.

keep himself, the Oversoul, and the primrose separate. What he called his "love unison" with the primrose, his going out in desire to it, was a matter of positive and negative vegetable polarity, not to be confused with the ladylike devotion of earlier nature lovers.[53] His theory of love seemed at once to preserve the independence of the flower and his own singularity. Jealous of impairing it, hating the thought of being part of a tradition while hunting for one to cling to, Lawrence labored the distinction between himself and Wordsworth, which, like those made in controversies among the Protestant sects, fails to mark an important difference.

Lawrence wrote a sequence of poems called "Birds, Beasts and Flowers." The order in which he listed these representatives of the living universe is significant in that birds and beasts claimed even more of his love than the flowers. He could not see why some people, confronted with a bird, wonder if it is edible.[54] Nor could he understand why other people think a god in heaven worth two in the bush. Shelley's transcendental affection for fowls, like Joyce Kilmer's for trees, was congenial to Lawrence. But to him birds and four-footed beasts meant something more: the chance of animal polarity. His little brown hen in New Mexico, his cat, the ram, snake, chipmunk, and tiger had this meaning, along with cock and bull. When he looked upon them, his thoughts far from food, he felt connected and heard the voice of the Holy Ghost.[55] Indeed, the tiger seemed to him to be the "Holy Ghost with

[53] *Porcupine*, pp. 168–75, 183, 229; *Phoenix*, p. 23.
[54] "Man Is a Hunter" in *Phoenix; Porcupine*, p. 234.
[55] *Porcupine*, pp. 138–39, 204–6, 231–32, 234; *Fantasia*, pp. 56–57, 154; *Letters*, p. 591; *Phoenix*, pp. 3, 40.

ice-shining whiskers." [56] Despite this fearful symmetry,
not tiger or even beaver, but the more domestic cat, bull,
cock, and horse served to symbolize the living universe
in *The Rainbow, Women in Love, The Plumed Serpent,*
and "The Man Who Died." Somers of *Kangaroo* com-
municates, as he sits in the bush, with big, handsome
birds, who sit waiting, "waiting the contact." [57] In the
zoo at Sydney he feeds peppermints to the kangaroos, ac-
cepts the glances of their "big, dark, prominent Aus-
tralian eyes, so aged in consciousness, with a fathomless,
dark, fern-age gentleness and gloom," and feels tender
and dark as he considers their blood. "It wasn't love he
felt for them, but a dark, animal tenderness, and another
sort of consciousness, deeper than human." [58] Lawrence's
soberest heroines contemplate symbolical snakes; one of
his heroes is less man than fox, diffusing, as he trots, a
foxy odor; the young peasant in "Sun" had "that wild
animal faculty"; [59] only villains, like Rico, are unbestial.
To illustrate animal love in *St. Mawr,* the novel most concerned with this subject, Lawrence chose the horse, [60]
which of all four-footed creatures, perhaps, is least un-
suitable in a love story addressed to the common reader.
By easy examples of horse and horse, man and horse, man
and woman, woman and horse, the reader is led to understand that in Lawrence's ark the animals paired. The
heroine of *St. Mawr* is saved from disconnection in the

[56] *Porcupine,* p. 235.
[57] *Kangaroo,* pp. 92–93. Cf. unsuccessful attempt on bird, *ibid.,* pp.
198–99.
[58] *Ibid.,* pp. 380–81. Cf. poem "Kangaroo," *Collected Poems,* II, 271.
[59] *Tales,* p. 754.
[60] For horse cf. *Apocalypse,* pp. 97–98; *Letters,* pp. 591–92; *Fantasia,*
pp. 56–57, 81, 154, 155. Lawrence was on intimate terms with his own
horse, according to Mabel Dodge Luhan, *Lorenzo in Taos,* p. 169.

flood and is swept into the ark by the "black fiery flow
. . . gushing from the darkness" of her horse, not to mention his groom.[61]

Many have wondered why Lawrence and his heroines
were fascinated by peasants, gipsies, grooms, and gamekeepers. E. T. says that, as far as she knows, Lawrence met
a gamekeeper only once. There was nothing attractive
about his solitary keeper, who caught the young poet
trespassing on a preserve near Nottingham and brutally
took away his flowers. The reason for his later interest
must be sought elsewhere, but it need be sought neither
long nor far. He liked gamekeepers and grooms as heroes
of his stories because they are close to nature. The peasants in George Sand's novels, of which he was extremely
fond,[62] or Wordsworth's rustics and children of nature
may have given Lawrence a hint or a pattern for his no
less natural men. Wordsworth's Lucy, who was so close
to sun, shower, and the scenery that vital feelings of delight swelled her bosom beyond repair, illustrates connection with nature. Of tougher stuff and very manly,
but otherwise not dissimilar, Lawrence's grooms and
gamekeepers, who are connected with sun, shower, birds,
horses, and trees, illustrate polarity with nature. No likelier saviours of unpolarized heroines can be imagined.
By establishing a connection first with the gamekeeper,
the heroine is led naturally, through his connections, to

[61] Jack of *The Boy in the Bush* is attracted to grooms and horsy
men (p. 213), and he enjoys polarity with his horse which enjoys polarity
with a mare (pp. 379, 382–83).

[62] *Letters*, p. 468. Lawrence had read *François le champi, Villemer,*
and *Les Maîtres Sonneurs.* He appears to have borrowed these books
and others from J. Middleton Murry. M. Seillière has traced the George
Sand influence.

all vital things. The first of these husbandmen, the game-keeper in *The White Peacock*, has only a symbolic function. Without a heroine to save, this follower of Rousseau saves his children from civilization. But the two grooms who attend to the wants of the horse St. Mawr, with whom they are polarized, have a better opportunity. Symbolically-named Phoenix, the Indian groom, and Lewis, the dark little Welsh groom, lead Mrs. Witt and Lady Lou through horses to all nature. Mellors, the saviour of Lady Chatterley, is close to pheasants and forget-me-nots, but his interest in four-footed creatures seems to be the secret of his success. To Lady Chatterley he says: "I'm used to horses, and cows, though they are very female, have a soothing effect on me. When I sit with my head in her side, milking, I feel very solaced.' " [63]

The nature of Lawrence's no less virtuous relationship with Susan should now be plain. As he milked her or gazed into her eyes, he felt neither intimate nor personal. He and she remained as individual as he and the primrose had. Yet her "cowy desirableness" excited his desire; and by desire, or the centrifugal and centripetal energy flowing among creatures and things to give them life, he was connected with her. His life was "widened and deepened in connection with her life," [64] and he was consummated with the living universe she congenially

[63] *Lady Chatterley*, p. 361.

[64] *Porcupine*, p. 234. Lawrence failed to find perfect polarity with his dog Bibbles, who wanted to merge with him ("Bibbles," *Collected Poems*, II, 274) or who loved others too well. In *A Poet and Two Painters*, pp. 160–77, Knud Merrild tells how Lawrence fell into a jealous rage upon finding Bibbles in another's lap. Lawrence pursued, caught, and repeatedly kicked his dog in the belly. He was intolerant of Judases. The Honorable Dorothy Brett tells of Lawrence's cruelty to a dung beetle, whose rich accumulation the poet maliciously removed.

represented. Through her he received power from the Unseen and did it reverence. "I accomplish nothing," he said, "not even my own fulfilled existence, unless I go forth, delicately, desirous, and find the mating of my desire; even if it be only the sky itself, and trees, and the cow Susan . . ." [65] In an early essay he confessed that he saw tragedy in every cow.[66] This is just as well; for had he seen comedy or milk alone, there would have been nothing to say.

[65] *Porcupine,* pp. 186–87. For Susan see also *ibid.,* pp. 133, 161–87, 233–34; *Letters,* pp. 636, 637.

[66] *Phoenix,* p. 82.

CHAPTER FOUR

SERMONS IN THE STONE AGE

PEASANT and gamekeeper were the best Europe had
to offer to one who sought the well-connected, and
Lawrence accepted the offering with gratitude; but however exemplary the gamekeeper, however familiar with
the trees and cows, he preserved only traces of better polarities in the past. Starting with these traces, Lawrence
searched for the gamekeeper's original in books about
ancient man, by whose example he had even higher hopes
of saving Europe from civilization and of leading it forward by leading it back. Back to nature came to mean
'way back to nature, to that communion with the sun
and flowers which early man enjoyed. Lawrence's favorite
world was antediluvian; his second choice was the world
of Egypt and Chaldea before 2000 B. C.,[1] and, failing that,
he contented himself with the vestiges of glory which he
discovered in the archaic societies of Etruscans, Hindus,
Aztecs, and Mrs. Mabel Dodge Luhan's Indians. The recovery of the living worshipful universe of these fortunate men was the aim of most of Lawrence's later essays
and novels, especially *The Plumed Serpent, Apocalypse,*
and *Etruscan Places.*

  There are many names for what Lawrence was, as I
have said before, but here it is fitting to call him a primitivist. Indeed, he is one of the completest specimens of a
type not uncommon during the last two hundred years.

[1] *Phoenix,* pp. 298, 769; *Apocalypse,* pp. 73–74.

Primitivism has been defined by Webster and by Professor Lovejoy [2] as a belief in the excellence of early or bucolic man because he was or is closer to nature than civilized man. An esteem for the virtue and innocence of such children of nature has appeared frequently, but most often at periods of over-ripe civilization. The natural, the odorous, and the brutish have the greatest appeal in the world to a polite and artificial society. Playing savage is a civilized diversion, and the appearance of primitivism today in the work of Lawrence and others is proof, in spite of evidence to the contrary, that we are very civilized, perhaps decadent. At such times queens carry milkpails, and poets their sensibilities, to the cows.

Since plumbing is also a sign, though not a necessary accompaniment, of civilization, it follows that primitivism and plumbing have often appeared together, the one best understood, perhaps, as surfeit with the other. The Palace of Minos, with its elaborate drains and cisterns, also housed the Minotaur. Rome of the twelve Caesars, with its apartment houses of many floors, its baths, its sumptuous vomitories, delighted in the arena, the Golden Age, and the virtues of the Germans. The eighteenth century, alone of primitivistic periods, was almost destitute of plumbing; for the rococo baths and the other conveniences of the palace seem hardly worth the mention. But recent times again display the customary signs of civilization. As Lawrence departed for his mountain in New Mexico, he condemned the pipes and the taps of America. [3]

[2] In his Foreword to Lois Whitney, *Primitivism and the Idea of Progress* (Baltimore, Johns Hopkins, 1934).

[3] *Classic American Literature*, p. viii. The heroine of *The Virgin*

The primitivism, if not the plumbing, of the eighteenth century is so much like our own in nature and origin that it should be considered in any discussion of more recent artificial savagery. As Professor Hoxie Neale Fairchild says,[4] the eighteenth century, too far gone in civilization for the comfort of some men, imagined an ideal past or an exotic present from which noble savages emerged to lead man back to innocence and instinct by their sermons and example. To an age forgetful of man's nature and ignorant of the flowers, civilized authors presented Laplanders, Aztecs, Negroes, American Indians, and South Sea Islanders, elevated above the actual and inflated by monitory heat. William Collins admired the superstitious Highlander; and Joseph Warton found relief from the amenities of Oxford in a hunt, no less enthusiastic for being sedentary, for the "boar and tiger through savannahs wild" of Georgia, perhaps, or Carolina. Warton's hunt is no more incredible than his Indian. The noble savage was never more than a moralist's device or a pleasing fancy, but as the convention grew it hid the actual savage even from those who were acquainted with him. In his *Letters from an American Farmer*, 1782, Crèvecœur pictured the redskin as more congenial than the white man, with whom he preferred to be after the redskin had burned his farm. Many years later the declining convention was still strong enough to

---

and the Gipsy, who abhors "indoor sanitation and . . . bathrooms," flees to her primitive gipsy, and a symbolical flood destroys the rectory, bathroom and all: *Tales*, p. 1050.

[4] *The Noble Savage* (New York, Columbia University Press, 1928). I am indebted to Professor Fairchild for my eighteenth-century illustrations.

make the natives of Herman Melville's valley of Typee
seem noble savages rather than Marquesans. During the
latter eighteenth and early nineteenth centuries, for
those whose fancies declined to wander too far from home
the peasant or the child became a substitute for the savage and was as useful for correcting civilization. In *Sand-
ford and Merton,* 1783–89, for example, Thomas Day
looked with equal favor on Laplanders, Indians, Negroes, and English peasants. The hero of Thomas Holcroft's *Anna of St. Ives,* 1792, is a baron's gardener's son,
who despises rank and riches, loves the baron's daughter,
and wants to retire to a society of savages in America. Not
unlike these creatures, Wordsworth's shepherds, leech-
gatherers, beggars, reapers, and children revealed the
benefits of nature to an unnatural society.

During the past fifty years a revival of interest in the
primitive as well as in other forms of the exotic has affected the arts, especially music, painting, and sculpture.
Moralists have pointed out that our popular music is
Negroid in origin and in character. Even more pompous
music such as Stravinsky's *Sacre du printemps* attempts
to capture the beat of the tom-tom and to suggest one
knows not what strange rites of aborigines. Stravinsky
composes for the ballet, and the ballet, as Arthur Symons
says, is at once artificial and primitive. The vogue of
African and geometrical sculpture, beginning in the
early years of this century and culminating in Gaudier-
Brzeska, Brancusi, and the French Colonial Exposition,
has largely determined the character of abstract and ex-
pressionistic painting from cubism through surrealism.
Under this influence as well as under that of Cézanne and

of Henri Rousseau,[5] whose landscapes are primitive in two senses of the word, Picasso advanced through cubes, newspaper clippings, and feeble-minded monoliths to bones embracing on a shore. The vistas of Dali are seen, he says, with the unconscious and the savage eye. Musing among the cubes, T. E. Hulme, the classical Bergsonist, hailed the new abstract art as primitive, religious, and fatal to humanism.

In literature the fashion of primitivism has been relatively inconspicuous. During the nineties, William Butler Yeats announced that it was time for man to begin ascending the path he had been descending since pre-Homeric times.[6] Much less certain of the innocence of these times, Arthur Machen was fascinated by Celtic antiquities, by mound and axe and ornament, which he interpreted according to the diabolism of his own period. Certain poems by Kipling, Robinson Jeffers, Carl Sandburg, and Vachel Lindsay, the books on the South Seas by Gauguin, O'Brien, and others, and the monotonous prose of Gertrude Stein show traces of primitivism or are closely connected with it. Edith Sitwell recently explained to critics who had accused her of being childish and artificial that she is really a primitivist, a simple, serious, spiritual, and inelegant creature, who, with the senses of a savage, is trying to see something beyond this world.[7] Miss Sitwell, whose prose and verse have faith-

[5] Lawrence possessed a print of Rousseau's lion and Arab picture: "The Unpublished Letters of D. H. Lawrence to Max Mohr," *T'ien Hsia Monthly*, I (August, 1935), 22. For primitivism in recent art see Robert J. Goldwater, *Primitivism in Modern Painting* (New York, Harper, 1938).

[6] "The Autumn of the Body," *Essays* (New York, Macmillan, 1924).

[7] "Some Notes on My Own Poetry," *The London Mercury*, Vol. XXXI

fully reflected the passing interests of other people, is anything but unfashionable, and her announcement is at least historically significant. However meager the other evidence of literary primitivism, literature possesses in D. H. Lawrence the most conspicuous primitivist of our times, a man whose nostalgic savagery exceeds that of his rivals not only in letters but in music and painting as well and one whose ideal unites the qualities of the eighteenth-century savage with those of a more recent model.

The primitivism of Lawrence resembles that of his eighteenth-century predecessor in that it also followed large developments of rationalism and science. Unable to adjust their emotions to Newton or Darwin, to cities and dark Satanic mills, Lawrence and the man of the eighteenth century alike turned to the savage as the embodiment of instinct, feeling, spirit, intuition, all that nature had given mankind, all that civilization had destroyed. As Lawrence's eighteenth-century predecessor discovered forgotten nature in the savage, he also anticipated Lawrence in finding a quarrel between nature and intellect and, taking the part of nature, also made an offensive weapon of the savage. Reasonable men, both then and now, faced with the evils attendant upon over-rapid material and intellectual changes, might suggest governmental regulation or better sewers; but the cult of the intuitive savage, the response of Lawrence and earlier men of feeling to such changes, had a more sentimental value.

(March, 1935). T. S. Eliot's use of primitive materials in *The Waste Land* is not, of course, primitivistic, however indicative it may be of contemporary interest in anthropology.

Lawrence's savage differs from that of the eighteenth-century sentimentalist, however, in that Lawrence for his ideas of the natural man drew upon sources of information unknown to earlier times. The enthusiast of the eighteenth century read books of travel and exploration, such as accounts of the South Seas by Hawkesworth or Cook, and, elevating what he found in these accounts by the aid of fancy and purpose, produced an amiable creature who would have been eaten for supper in the Sandwich Islands. Men like Southey, who liked Aztecs or more primitive redskins, read the books of Bernal Diaz and of other adventurers or travelers in America. But Lawrence drew upon the works of the anthropologists, who since the 1870's have changed our conception of the savage and made the earlier notions untenable. He also used the psychoanalysts, who have provided another approach to the mind of ancient man. Colonial expansion in the nineteenth century and fuller accounts by historians, travelers, and explorers gave him a better opportunity to know the habits of the natural man. Although Lawrence also improved by the aid of theory, purpose, and sentiment the facts he took from his sources, anthropology gave his savage a new demeanor and a different nobility.

Nature, too, with which the natural man must keep in harmony if he is to remain natural, had changed since the eighteenth century. Wordsworth's friendly English world of daffodils and primroses, immune from hippopotamus or termite, gave way during the nineteenth century before a world which seemed uncongenial, indifferent, harsh. Even before the struggle for existence was officially announced, poets like Matthew Arnold, sensing the change, had seen nature cruel. Thomas Hardy's world was one of fungus and mildew and of cold grey stones upon which poets now declined to sit for fear of parasites.

In the preceding chapter, while discussing Lawrence's connection with Wordsworthian nature worship, I said that the differences, apart from poetry, between the two poets are like those which distinguish one variety of Protestant from another, matters of accident rather than of importance. Here I am concerned with those differences. Lawrence belonged to the tradition of Wordsworth in that he worshiped nature and felt connection with it to be of benefit, and it is plain that he was inspired in part by Wordsworth and his school, but the nature with which Lawrence wanted to be connected was different from that of his master. Lawrence had read Darwin, naturalists such as Bates and W. H. Hudson,[8] poets like Hardy. Science had intervened between Wordsworth and Lawrence to make nature seem alien, as it had seemed to Hardy, but Lawrence is closer to Wordsworth than to Hardy in that he still found nature to be worshipful and still maintained Wordsworthian relations with it, however forbidding it now appeared to be. Lawrence's relationship or polarity had a negative as well as a positive current. The negative is a recognition of the hostility of nature; the positive, of its Wordsworthian attractiveness. Lawrence is a lesser Wordsworth, dealing in the familiar way with a nature brought up to date by the new biology. The devotion to the object remained the same; the character of the object differed.

[8] *Classic American Literature,* p. 40.

The heroine of *St. Mawr,* whose relationship with nature becomes impeccable, encounters the new nature in New Mexico. As she contemplates the chipmunks, she feels alien and constrained to abandon her old notions of universal love. "The wild life, even the life of the trees and flowers, seemed one bristling, hair-raising tussle." The cactus seems, as indeed it is, menacing to one accustomed to recline on English lawns. The very hills appear to be malevolent. Yet it is with this nature that she finds peace and connection.[9] Somers, in Australia, feels the inhumanity of the bush and resents the indifference of the birds, yet finally balances negative by positive polarity. One day he sees a horrible octopus in a seaside pool. Wordsworth had never confronted the problem of such a natural embrace.[10]

Biology, then, as well as anthropology, accounts for the nature of Lawrence's natural man and for the differences between him and the noble savage. It was fortunate for the pride Lawrence took in his originality that, although he was familiar with the tradition of the noble savage, he could see only these differences. His attitude toward his primitivistic predecessors, like his attitude toward most men whom he resembled or to whom he was indebted, was hostile and contemptuous. As a lad, he had read Cooper's *Leatherstocking Tales* and was consumed with the desire to encounter noble savages in the forests of "Cooperstown on Lake Champlain." [11] Later he read

[9] *St. Mawr* in *Tales,* pp. 680–83; cf. *Tales,* pp. 704, 711, 714–15.

[10] *Kangaroo,* pp. 199, 373, 383, 389. Somers sees maggots in a dead rabbit: "Writhe then, Life, he seemed to say to the things—and he no longer saw its sickeningness." *Ibid.,* p. 267. Cf. *Sea and Sardinia,* p. 83: a fisherman takes advantage of the loves of the octopus.

[11] *Classic American Literature,* pp. 54, 72–73, 79.

Crèvecœur's *Letters from an American Farmer,* Melville's *Typee* and *Omoo,* Weaver's *Melville,*[12] the works of Bernardin de Saint-Pierre, Chateaubriand, François Le Vaillant, and the once-more-misinterpreted Rousseau.[13] After he had read his anthropology and biology and had met Mr. Luhan, the Indian husband of Mabel Dodge Luhan, Lawrence issued essays on Cooper, Crèvecœur, and Melville to express his disillusionment with the noble savage. Cooper and Crèvecœur, he said, evaded the actual or concealed it under ideal and intellectual myths. For a time he had been taken in by their lies about a sweet and innocent nature and a magnanimous Indian, but now he knew that these civilized primitivists were no better than Marie Antoinette with her milk-pail and as far from reality. Real nature, Lawrence continued, is fierce, the American landscape is devilish, the Indian is as alien and inhospitable as the cactus and as full of a dark, mindless life which only Lawrence could know. With such savages and with such nature, he said, we cannot live on friendly terms as Crèvecœur vainly imagined. But Lawrence, who always allowed sectarian differences to impair his vision, was unable to see that he and Crèvecœur were alike. However different the aspect of Lawrence's savage, however unfriendly, he was but a didactic symbol, and it was in this capacity that Crèvecœur's friendly savage had flourished. Neither Crèvecœur nor Lawrence greatly desired to live with his savage. They wanted to teach by him,

[12] According to an unpublished letter from Middleton Murry to Miss Louise Koegel, one of my students. Mr. Murry presented Lawrence with a copy of Crèvecœur during the early years of the war: *Son of Woman,* p. 206.

[13] *Classic American Literature,* p. 36. Le Vaillant wrote *Voyage dans l'intérieur de l'Afrique,* 1790.

and by his example to improve the condition of man.

"I am so tired," said Lawrence, "of being told that I want mankind to go back to the condition of savages." [14] In his essay on *Typee,* he condemned as renegades those sophisticated white men who betrayed their whiteness and the progress of the world by their desire to go native. Neither Melville nor Gauguin, he continued, had found happiness among the idyllic Polynesians; nor could any white man of our time.[15] Though we cannot go back to the savage or to the past, we must learn from the savage and the past in order to revive the present.[16] Civilization has become too tame, he said, and we must untame ourselves, cultivate the feelings, "get back to the roots again for a new start," and "sow wild seed again." [17] Sowing his wild seed, Lawrence pressed forward, renewing the present, advancing toward the future by the aid of a savage past. "Every profound new movement," he said, "makes a great swing also backwards to some older, half-forgotten way of consciousness." [18] The hero of one of his stories expressed the same idea more neatly: ". . . my desire to go onwards takes me back a little." [19] Lawrence seems to have thought that going back to the savage for the purpose of progress exempted him from the charge of primi-

[14] *Phoenix,* p. 194; cf. *Assorted Articles,* pp. 204–5, and *Mornings in Mexico,* pp. 104–5.

[15] *Classic American Literature,* pp. 74, 196–204; cf. *Kangaroo,* p. 390: Somers is not an enemy of civilization, as some said, but only an enemy of its evils, machines and mind. Cf. *ibid.,* p. 231: Somers is accused of being a traitor to intelligence.

[16] *Phoenix,* pp. 31, 99; *Letters,* p. 605; Earl Brewster, *D. H. Lawrence, Reminiscences and Correspondence,* p. 213.

[17] *Phoenix,* p. 758; cf. *Apocalypse,* p. 173.

[18] *Apocalypse,* p. 50; cf. *Letters,* p. 362, and *Classic American Literature,* p. 204.

[19] *Tales,* p. 876.

tivism. But the typical primitivist of the eighteenth century, such as Bage or Holcroft, was also intent on progress; and Rousseau reared Émile in a savage way not to make him a savage but to make him a better and more natural citizen of a superior civilization.

What we could learn from the savage for our improvement was, of course, that dark relationship with the living universe which among the people of Europe only the gamekeeper or the peasant enjoys. But to Lawrence the modern savage was not altogether satisfactory. Though closer to nature than most of us, his unfriendly Indian had degenerated from nobler ancestors who had been much closer. The modern savage, however, preserved tribal echoes from "away back . . . before the Flood," [20] and he remained of considerable value as a clue to the greater past. As he taught polarity to the civilized by the aid of the vestigial redskin, Lawrence looked through him to his "darker" original, the archaic man of Mexico, Egypt, and Atlantis.

He found archaic and primitive man not in Egypt, India, or Tahiti, for Romans, Englishmen, and disease had preceded him to these places, still less in Mexico, for Spaniards had preceded him there, but in books by anthropologists, archaeologists, psychoanalysts, and historians, to which he was devoted from 1913 to the time of his death. He was on familiar terms with Frazer's *Golden Bough*, a work which affected him even more than it has most of the bookish men of our time.[21] In 1913 he read Jane Harrison's *Ancient Art and Ritual*, in 1916 Ed-

[20] *Phoenix*, pp. 145–46.
[21] *Fantasia*, pp. 7–8, 10; *Apocalypse*, p. 184.

ward Tylor's *Primitive Culture,* both of which pleased him immensely, and in 1918 *The Voice of Africa,* a study of Yoruban vestiges of Atlantis, by Leo Frobenius.[22] M. Seillière complains that Frobenius is the only German, save for Mrs. Lawrence and Freud of course, with whom Lawrence admitted acquaintance; but haste may have kept this scholar from noticing that Lawrence says he read Jung in 1918, probably his *Psychology of the Unconscious,* a study of primitive myth and symbol.[23] In 1919 Lawrence borrowed Prescott's *Peru* from Katherine Mansfield; [24] in 1916 he had read two accounts of ancient Egypt: Gaston Maspero's *Égypte,* as Mrs. Julian Huxley, who lent it to Lawrence, has kindly informed me, and a history lent him by Lady Ottoline Morrell, who remembered neither author nor title.[25] It is likely from his references to Chaldea and Babylonia that Lawrence knew Maspero's longer history of Egypt, which includes accounts of these countries. He probably read the six-volume *History of Egypt,* 1898–1905, or the shorter *Religion of Egypt,* 1906, by Sir William Matthew Flinders Petrie, perhaps the foremost English authority, with whose writings, if we may judge from a casual allusion in *Kangaroo,* Lawrence was familiar.[26] His reference in *Apocalypse* to reading translations of stories from the Egyptian almost certainly means that he was acquainted with Petrie's *Egyptian Tales,* 1899.[27] He also read Gilbert Murray on the ancient Greeks,[28] and after 1920 he looked

[22] *Letters,* pp. 149, 164–65, 344, 439.   [23] *Ibid.,* p. 458.
[24] *Ibid.,* p. 468; unpublished letter from Middleton Murry to Miss Louise Koegel.
[25] *Letters,* pp. 314, 318, 322.   [26] *Kangaroo,* p. 49.
[27] *Apocalypse,* p. 85.   [28] *Letters,* p. 344.

through many books, which I shall refer to later, on Egypt, India, Mexico, the Etruscans, and the early Iron Age.[29]

That such reading excited him is plain from the comment he made in 1916 on finishing a *History of the East*, which I have been unable to identify: ". . . something in me lights up and understands these old, dead peoples, and I love it: Babylon, Nineveh, Ashurbanipal, how one somehow suddenly understands it. And I cannot tell you the joy of ranging far back there . . ." [30] He came to regard the ancient Egyptians as the most fortunate of men. His letters and essays abound in references to totemism, fertility rituals, dying and reborn gods. The deities and the symbols of the ancients, Osiris, Ra, Thoth, Hermes, Ashtaroth, the ram, the mistletoe, and the bull of Mithras, assumed a spiritual significance in his mind.[31] Even the festival of Easter, which he had ceased to celebrate, began to take on meaning when he found it to have been the festival of rebirth and regeneration in all the old religions.[32] "I know there has to be a return to the older vision of life . . ." he said. "It needs some welling up of religious sources that have been shut down in us: a great *yielding* . . . to the darker, older unknown, and a reconciliation." [33] He knew that he had recaptured the worship of early man, which he proceeded to add, as still another element and perhaps the most important, to his

[29] *Ibid.*, p. 704; Brewster, *Reminiscences*, p. 163; Frieda Lawrence, *"Not I, but the Wind . . . ,"* p. 208.

[30] *Letters*, p. 318.

[31] *Fantasia*, pp. 10, 58, 100; *Porcupine*, pp. 83, 120, 139–40; *Phoenix*, p. 289; *Letters*, pp. 412, 558, 702–3; *Apocalypse*, pp. 93, 163; Brewster, *Reminiscences*, p. 227.

[32] *Phoenix*, pp. 288–89.   [33] *Letters*, p. 605.

developing religion of mindlessness and love. If Lawrence's system of worship with its authentic Easter seems less suitable to Nottingham than to Easter Island, one must remember that it is the nature of a private religion to be private.

As he descended through the ages in search of purer divinity, the religious man faced, with the patience of a stylite, the obstacle to his descent: he had almost no books of his own. Homeless, vagrant, rarely near a public library, he was compelled to depend upon his acquaintances and friends for the books he read. Yet his reading was enormous and for the most part in his fields of interest. He was fortunate in his friends, who owned and lent the books demanded by the fashionable taste; and during the war, the period of Lawrence's development, this taste demanded anthropology and archaeology as well as psychoanalysis.

An interest in scientific or scholarly works might seem odd in an enemy of science and mind; but Lawrence's approach to the books he borrowed was emotional rather than academic and not altogether incompatible with mindlessness. The inner light fell across the page and passion warmed the room. As he read the most discouraging books, he found affinities in spite of context. He came from each book with what his convictions, based more than he was aware upon previous books, had demanded; and as he borrowed the next, he hoped that it would "have something in it for me." [34] To Lady Ottoline Morrell he wrote in 1916: "I should like you to get me out of the library a history of early Egypt, before the Greeks: a

[34] *Ibid.,* p. 704.

book not too big, because I like to fill it in myself, and the contentions of learned men are so irritating." [35]

He did not attempt to conceal his irritation with the unimaginative works he condescended to misuse. He found Frobenius tiresome, Jane Harrison schoolmarmy, Frazer scientific. He said that historians and anthropologists had no understanding of early man, that works so rational and materialistic as theirs were without value, that he knew more about golden boughs than Frazer. To Frazer, he said, the ram was so much mutton, the bull so much beef, but to himself, as to the priests of religions which few modern men can understand, these beasts were mysteries.[36] Religion being right, science wrong, he was compelled to interpret in a liberal and religious way what he took from these materialists. "I have found hints, suggestions for what I say here," he admitted, "in all kinds of scholarly books . . . down to Fraser and his 'Golden Bough,' and even Freud and Frobenius. Even then I only remember hints—and I proceed by intuition." [37]

After 1915 Lawrence's essays and stories began to show a considerable debt to Frazer, Frobenius, and the historians. As early as 1912 Lawrence had confessed in a letter that he adored "a primeval feeling," [38] but after much reading he knew better what he had been talking about. "The Crown," 1915, contains references to Dionysus, Moloch, and Egyptian animal worship; "Education of

---

[35] *Ibid.,* p. 318.

[36] *Apocalypse,* pp. 85, 184; *Fantasia,* p. 10; *Mornings in Mexico,* p. 103; *Letters,* pp. 164–65, 318, 439, 619; *Porcupine,* pp. 232–33; *Kangaroo,* p. 331; *Phoenix,* p. 29; Brewster, *Reminiscences,* p. 227; Luhan, *Lorenzo in Taos,* pp. 138–40, 150, 310; Frederick Carter, *D. H. Lawrence and the Body Mystical,* pp. 17, 61; E. T., *Personal Record,* pp. 113, 122.

[37] *Fantasia,* pp. 7–8.   [38] *Letters,* p. 71.

the People" (written about 1920) has reference to the tree of life; *Movements in European History,* 1921, contains long passages, based apparently upon Frazer, concerning the Great Mother, the gods of fertility and the sun, and druidical worship of trees and mistletoe or the golden bough; *Fantasia* invokes the awful names of the Greeks, the Etruscans, and the Egyptians.[39] Birkin, of *Women in Love,* 1920, an enemy of cities, loves African sculpture for its "mystically sensual" character, the Russian ballet, and the paintings of Picasso. But to these contemporary examples of the primitive he prefers the ancient Egyptians, whom he makes his models in mindlessness, vitalism, and polarity. The Bohemians of Bloomsbury, strangely unfashionable for the moment, ridicule Birkin for wanting to go back to the savages. I said unfashionable because even Gerald, the civilized, likes to read books of anthropology.[40] Lilly, of *Aaron's Rod,* 1922, reads Frobenius to the music of Debussy: "His soul had the faculty of divesting itself of the moment, and seeking further, deeper interests. These old Africans! And Atlantis! Strange, strange wisdom of the Kabyles! Old, old dark Africa, and the world before the flood!" [41] This enemy of present civilization also loves Aztecs, South Sea Islanders, and Egyptians, "lost races . . . lost human ways of feeling and of knowing." [42] Count Dionys, of "The Ladybird," 1923, has much that is primitive about him besides his name. He is a devotee of the

---

[39] *Porcupine,* pp. 74, 83; *Phoenix,* p. 610; *Movements in European History,* pp. 59–60, 92; *Fantasia,* pp. 77, 100.

[40] *Women in Love,* pp. 82–83, 88, 102–3, 265, 288, 289, 291, 363–65, 437 ff., 511.

[41] *Aaron's Rod,* pp. 128–29.   [42] *Ibid.,* pp. 113, 309–10, 334, 345.

sun, he claims, and belongs to the age-old fire worshipers. His symbolic ladybird is an Egyptian scarab, a pre-Roman convenience which is far more natural than a sewer.[43]

As the author of these conceits wandered about, he kept an eye open for places where vestiges of the primitive might still be lingering or for men whom civilization had left unspoiled. He was delighted with Cornwall, whither he had retired during the war; for in this place above all other British places he could feel the past. The landscape was "primeval," suggesting the worship of stones, blood sacrifice, mistletoe, and all the mysteries of pre-Christian days. Here was something still untouched by mental consciousness and civilization. Snuffing druidical blood, he entered the ancient twilight, calling Tuatha De Danann to the spirits.[44] It was here that Somers, and Somers is but another name for Lawrence, crooned a Hebridean folk song, which pleased him because it had no meaning. "Ver mi hiu—ravo na la vo—" it went. "Ver mi hiu—ravo hovo i—." It was here that he met and loved John Thomas, the farmer, who appealed because he was half peasant and half Celt. From these delights Somers and Lawrence were removed by the police, not under Section XI of the Criminal Law Amendment Act of 1885 but under an act for the defense of the realm.[45]

Undismayed, and with a keener appetite for peasants, Lawrence went, as soon as he was permitted, to Italy,

[43] *Tales*, pp. 370, 406. In her memoir the Honorable Dorothy Brett tells of Lawrence's interest in the dung beetle.

[44] "Cornwall," said Lawrence in *Kangaroo*, p. 254, "is a country that makes a man psyche [*sic*]."

[45] *Kangaroo*, pp. 253, 254, 266–67, 275; see Luhan, *Lorenzo in Taos*, p. 51, on the farmer of Cornwall.

which, he thought, might lead him "back, back down the old ways of time." [46] On his earlier trip to Italy, as told in *Twilight in Italy*, 1916, he had observed the peasants with interest; on the second trip, as told in *Sea and Sardinia*, 1921, his hunt for the primitive peasant became an obsession. The peasants of Sicily proved to be corrupt and jeering; but those of Sardinia, a more backward place, were somewhat better, and Lawrence was able to find a few with the old blood-familiarity, suitably mindless, and with "dangerous thighs." [47] On the whole, however, he was disappointed; for the more aboriginal the peasant, the dirtier he was, and Lawrence had not counted on dirt. He had pictured an ideal peasant, noble and uncivilized, straight from the pages of George Sand. The actual peasant was disenchanting. Lawrence "cursed the degenerate aborigines. . . . 'Why don't you take it as it comes?'" asked Mrs. Lawrence. "'It's all life.'" [48] But Lawrence traveled with his ideals, insisting on his tea in the most unlikely places.

He shook the dirt of Sardinia from his feet in 1922 and, running from civilization and himself,[49] departed for Ceylon, where tea and the prospect of finding savages looked better. In Ceylon he stayed with his friend Earl Brewster, an American Buddhist, whose descriptions of the East had given Lawrence some hope. But India was also sordid, its climate impossible, its people separated

[46] *Sea and Sardinia*, p. 216.

[47] *Ibid.*, pp. 113, 116, 160, 250, 355. Cf. Lawrence's Introduction to Maurice Magnus, *Memoirs of the Foreign Legion*, p. 39, and *The Lost Girl*, pp. 321–72: the heroine's mindless peasant husband gives her "atavistic" sensations and fills her with nostalgia for the past.

[48] *Sea and Sardinia*, pp. 176, 177; cf. pp. 161–62, 171–73, 196.

[49] *Letters*, pp. 543, 556; *Kangaroo*, pp. 8, 168.

from him by a gulf even wider than he had found between himself and the peasants.[50] Instead of children of nature, Lawrence encountered the Prince of Wales. After a month of such discouragements, Lawrence departed in May for Australia. Here he found not aborigines but Europeans like himself, and the bush was too primitive, suggesting the fern age rather than the world of the Egyptian.[51] What was worse, in the house he rented by the shore near Sydney he found all the modern conveniences. A few months of this were enough. Pursued by the actual, he departed in the fall of 1922 for America. The boat stopped at Tahiti. Instead of children of nature, he met cinema people from the States. Feeling his soul disintegrate,[52] he continued his journey to New Mexico, whither he had been invited by Mrs. Mabel Dodge Luhan, who, having read *Sea and Sardinia,* thought that a peasant fancier would be able to endure the Indians with whom she preferred to reside. He had written to her of his hopes in the Indian, of finding something in Taos that he had failed to find in the East or in the world of white men.[53] But what he called his "savage pilgrimage" [54] had been for the moment too much for him, and upon arriving in New Mexico, as we have seen, he expressed in *Studies in Classic American Literature,* 1923, his passing disillusionment with the noble savage. It was this disillusionment together with his experiences in America and his reading in anthropology that caused

[50] Brewster, *Reminiscences,* p. 48; Luhan, *Lorenzo in Taos,* p. 18; *Sea and Sardinia,* pp. 161–62, 196.

[51] *Kangaroo,* pp. 198–201; cf. pp. 8, 169, and also *Letters,* pp. 547, 549.

[52] *Classic American Literature,* pp. 196, 203, 204, 206.

[53] Luhan, *Lorenzo in Taos,* pp. 6, 23.   [54] *Letters,* p. 562.

Lawrence to invent a new kind of ideal savage, through whom he might fathom the world of Egypt and Atlantis. "No men are so evil to-day as the idealists," he said in his essay on Melville. Two pages later, after a lapse of memory, he added: "Melville was, at the core, a mystic and an idealist. Perhaps, so am I." [55]

Almost immediately upon his arrival at Mrs. Luhan's home at Taos, his ideals began to revive under what he conceived to be the religious atmosphere of the place and the pious conduct of the aborigines. In his essay "New Mexico" he said: "I had looked over all the world for something that would strike *me* as religious." [56] He had investigated the primitive intensity of peasants in Cornwall, Bavaria, Italy, the ecstasy of the Buddhists in India, and the devil dances of Ceylon, which were religious enough, to be sure, but which had failed to involve *him*. He had been disappointed in Australia and Tahiti. But here in New Mexico he found at last that union of the religious and the primitive for which he had sought. He was at last freed from this era of mechanical progress and from the materialism and idealism of the present world. The blood sacrifice of the Druids had been pleasing but not up to that of the sun-loving Aztecs. "Ah, yes, in New Mexico the heart is sacrificed to the sun, and the human being is left stark, heartless, but undauntedly religious." [57] The descendants of the Aztecs, too, retained traces of a "vast old religion," far older than those of the Greeks, the Hindus, or even the Egyptians. "It is curious," he said, "that one should get a sense of living

[55] *Classic American Literature*, pp. 210, 212.
[56] *Phoenix*, p. 143.   [57] *Ibid.*

religion from the Red Indians, having failed to get it from Hindus or Sicilian Catholics or Cingalese." [58] Two essays of 1924, "Resurrection" and "On Being Religious," as well as *Mornings in Mexico* and *Reflections on the Death of a Porcupine,* gave similar expression to the sentiments inspired by the redskin.

However objectionable the Indian might sometimes be, however impossible the sentimentalist's dream of friendship with him,[59] he was an example for the paleface. For whether he was washing his long black hair or scalping an acquaintance, the Indian acknowledged the wonder of it all, and his religion was that by which the paleface might be saved.[60] The Indian maintains that all is god, not that god is in everything, as the pantheists hold, but that everything is alive, that rocks, sun, and trees are gods. Once, said Lawrence,

the whole life-effort of man was to get his life into direct contact with the elemental life of the cosmos, mountain-life, cloud-life, thunder-life, air-life, earth-life, sun-life. To come into immediate *felt* contact, and so derive energy, power, and a dark sort of joy. This effort into sheer naked contact, *without an intermediary or mediator,* is the root meaning of religion . . .[61]

This polytheistic religion of long ago, with its Protestant contempt of intermediary, happily combined Lawrence's theories of vitalism and relationship and fitted better than even he could have hoped into the pattern of his earlier sermons. But this was scarcely odd since, as he observed the festivals of the barbarous, he could not re-

58 *Ibid.,* pp. 142–45.
59 *Ibid.,* p. 147; *Mornings in Mexico,* pp. 104–5.
60 *Assorted Articles,* p. 67.   61 *Phoenix,* pp. 146–47.

frain from reading his preconceptions into them; and, years before, he had found in Frazer and Tylor the explanation of what he now observed. Under their influence he now discarded the word vitalism for one with connotations more primitive: animistic became the word to describe his devotion to the living universe. "This animistic religion," he wrote to Middleton Murry, "is the only live one . . ." [62]

The convert to animism found his ideal in the ceremonial dance. Dancing on the mesa among the prickly pears, the religious redskin drew his energies from the malevolent yet necessary powers of nature. By his soft, downward bird-tread he battled the living potencies of earth, sun, wind, and rain to win from them the strength to endure them, to grow corn, to rear children. Not so the paleface, who conquered the potencies by railroads, windmills, dams, and cisterns. Lawrence saw at once that the animistic dance was better than the windmill; for religion was right, science wrong. Moved to "unspeakable depths," he turned with awe to the dancer, who, in snatching energy from an alien, living universe, was obviously practicing positive and negative polarity, wooing the god-vibration in all things with the intensity of an Egyptian. It is true that Lawrence's first reaction to the dance, as expressed in a letter,[63] had been unfavorable; but his ideals soon intervened to create those unforgettable impressions of savage piety: "The Hopi Snake Dance," "The Dance of the Sprouting Corn," and "In-

[62] Letters, p. 610; cf. p. 604, and also Mornings in Mexico, pp. 147, 177, 178.
[63] Letters, pp. 607–10.

dians and Entertainment." [64] Other writers had been content to watch; but Lawrence, returning home in the evening, would dance the tread-dance with little bird-steps to the beat of Mr. Luhan's drum. [65]

Observation, practice, and the ideal of polarity helped Lawrence to see the meaning of what he saw; but, as I have said, Frazer and Tylor were also of considerable help. From them he learned, for example, that the Dance of the Sprouting Corn was the Easter ceremony of the resurrected vegetable. [66] His principal debt, however, was to a book he had read many years earlier, Jane Harrison's *Ancient Art and Ritual,* a study of the ancient Greek ceremonial dance. What he learned from this work about the religious, non-recreational character of the primitive dance he applied to the restless animists of New Mexico.

At Taos, Lawrence also enjoyed a sedentary connection with the universe of the ancients. In "Pan in America" he tells how he sat before a pine tree and aboriginally drew from it the Pan-power with which man had been filled before machines debauched the potencies of earth and sky. The tree vibrated into his soul, his soul into the tree, as he exclaimed after the manner of the animist: "Give me of your power, then, oh tree!" [67] The savage had been right about the golden bough, the tree of life. And horses too: how right he had been about the

[64] All in *Mornings in Mexico.* See particularly pp. 131, 135, 138, 147, 148, 159, 172, 173, 177; cf. *Phoenix,* pp. 145, 146–47. Cf. peasant dance: "The Dance," *Twilight in Italy,* pp. 175 ff.

[65] *Letters,* p. 604.   [66] *Mornings in Mexico,* p. 127.

[67] *Phoenix,* pp. 24–26. Cf. his earlier druidical tree-worship: *Fantasia,* p. 37, and *Movements in European History,* p. 92.

horse. Some years later Lawrence was to say: "Horses, always horses! How the horse dominated the mind of the early races. . . . Far back, far back in our dark soul the horse prances." [68] As Lawrence's horse pranced through the back yard at Taos, Mrs. Luhan was struck with the connection between man and beast, and the horseman regretted that even the tree-conscious Indian had degenerated so far as to have forgotten the horse. [69]

It was at Taos that Lawrence met Susan. In Australia, Somers had attempted a cow; but although he had fed her pumpkins, he had met with no success. Like her native bush, she had remained cold, indifferent. [70] But here in Taos, among the pine trees and the dancers, the atmosphere proved more congenial. For Susan was more to Lawrence than a timeless representative of the living universe; she was also the symbolic, worshipful beast of ancient man, Lawrence's equivalent of the ram, of the Mithraic bull, of the Aztec snake. His relationship with her was that of the Egyptian with his beetle, of the Druid with his sacred oak or his mistletoe. "In the great ages," he said, "man had vital relation . . . with the cow, the lion, the bull, the cat, the eagle, the beetle, the serpent. And beyond these, with narcissus and anemone, mistletoe and oak-tree . . ." [71] As he looked upon Susan with reverence, Lawrence could not but recall the bull of Mithras: "Is not this my life, this throbbing of the bull's blood in my blood?" As he looked more attentively upon her, he thought of the cave man's pure relationship with the deer and the mammoth. [72] Such thoughts are not to

[68] *Apocalypse*, p. 97; cf. *Letters*, pp. 590–93.
[69] Luhan, *Lorenzo in Taos*, p. 169; *Phoenix*, p. 147.
[70] *Kangaroo*, p. 210.   [71] *Porcupine*, p. 231.
[72] *Ibid.*, pp. 83, 140–41, 231, 232–34. Norman Douglas's attitude toward

be wondered at in a reader of Frobenius; for in his collection at Frankfort that anthropologist displayed prehistoric paintings of men engaged in worship of the
sacred cow.[73] As Lawrence milked Susan, his thoughts
were directed by Frazer, perhaps, to the Great Mother
of early man. "This great mother," he had said, "is like
the gentle cow which supports our life. Even the Mother
of Jesus had with her in the stable the cows of peace and
plenty . . ." [74] Thoughts like these are only natural to
the devout reader of anthropology, as similar vagaries
had been natural to the eighteenth-century primitivist,
the reader of travelers' tales, who, praising the state of
nature, had provoked from Dr. Johnson not the smile of
pity but the paragraph of contempt: "Do not allow yourself, Sir, to be imposed upon by such gross absurdity.
It is sad stuff; it is brutish. If a bull could speak, he
might as well exclaim,— Here am I with this cow and
this grass; what being could enjoy greater felicity?" [75]
The civilized Dr. Johnson, who remained stubbornly
hostile to some of the products of civilization, would
have been unable to see that Susan is as much the creature of the civilized fancy as that wooden cow of Crete,
which gratified its architect, amused its mistress, and en-

---

the cow, especially toward Catherine, the resurrected cow, was irreverent: *Old Calabria* (New York, Modern Library, 1928). From this can
be seen why Douglas and Lawrence were incompatible. See Lawrence's
Introduction to Magnus, *Memoirs of the Foreign Legion;* Douglas,
D. H. Lawrence and Maurice Magnus.

[73] Photographs of these were exhibited in 1937 at the Museum of
Modern Art, New York. One picture, of about 9000 B. C., shows religious
men dancing about a cow. The cow is worshiped today by certain
African tribes.

[74] *Movements in European History*, p. 60.

[75] Quoted in Fairchild, *Noble Savage*, p. 334.

larged the understanding, perhaps, of *la fille de Minos et de Pasiphaë*.

Cow and pine tree, drum and dance were very good, but New Mexico and even Mexico, to which Lawrence went in 1923, fell short of his ideals. After all, the actual Indian was degenerate; and Lawrence felt that he had looked in vain for a barbarous nation to restore us to vitality.[76] But he had discovered clues and primitive places. If, following these clues, he could people these places with a few chosen spirits, "as wise as serpents"—Middleton Murry, for example, and Koteliansky, Mrs. Carswell, and the Honorable Dorothy Brett—how happy he would be as he directed their dance around Susan. As he had once proposed religious colonies in Florida and among the Andes,[77] so on a visit to England late in the same year he proposed a primitive community in Taos or Mexico. Years before this, Coleridge had said:

What I dared not expect from constitutions of governments and whole nations I hoped from religion and a small company of chosen individuals, and formed a plan, as harmless as it was extravagant, of trying the experiment of human perfectibility on the banks of the Susquehannah; where our little society . . . was to have combined the innocence of the Patriarchal Age with the knowledge and general refinements of European culture . . .[78]

However similar Pantisocracy might appear, Lawrence dismissed it with disdain;[79] for his own scheme was unsentimental, his refuge Mexico, not the Susquehanna. To the beat of the drum he would lead his followers to

[76] *Fantasia*, p. 163.
[77] *Letters*, pp. 215, 220, 221, 278, 298, 375, 420.
[78] *The Friend*, quoted in Fairchild, *Noble Savage*, p. 196.
[79] *Classic American Literature*, p. 33.

what Coleridge had never imagined: the authentic Egyptian darkness. The betrayal of this dream by all except the Honorable Dorothy Brett forced Lawrence to create an imaginary community. *The Plumed Serpent,* 1926, represents the primitive religious Utopia he had been denied. Immediately upon completing this novel, he said: ". . . one can live so intensely with one's characters and the experiences one creates or records, it is a life in itself, far better than the vulgar thing people *call* life . . ." [80]

In *The Plumed Serpent,* by far his best novel as well as the outstanding example of primitivism in our time, Lawrence used the myths of the Aztecs to carry his message. His first response to Mexico and its gods, as expressed in the essay "Au Revoir, U.S.A.," had been unfavorable; but he soon discovered that, no matter how repulsive the Aztecs had been, they had also preserved traces of a sublimer past, that their Quetzalcoatl was really a survivor from this past, and that he was still useful. Filled with second thoughts, Lawrence made Mrs. Lawrence do Aztec embroidery. What is more, he told in *The Plumed Serpent* how Don Ramon and Don Cipriano, the one a graduate of Columbia, the other of Oxford, but nevertheless Laurentian animists, revived what they called the religion of the pre-Aztec god Quetzalcoatl and, by the aid of drum, dance, sermon, symbol, and the destruction of socialists, papists, and engineers, established primitive nature-worship as the religion of Mexico. Animism, polarity, and the dances of Taos [81]

[80] *Letters,* p. 638.

[81] Mrs. Luhan has pointed out in *Lorenzo in Taos* that the dances and drums of *The Plumed Serpent* come from New Mexico, not Mexico,

account for much of the cult of Quetzalcoatl. But Lawrence shows acquaintance with the Aztec myths, which he improved in the light of his understanding; and Frazer, Tylor, and Harrison do not explain his knowledge. The source of his Mexican learning was a problem.

Without much trouble I found from allusions in his works and from correspondence with Mrs. Luhan, Witter Bynner, and Mrs. Lawrence that, while or before he was in New Mexico and Mexico, Lawrence read Prescott's *Conquest of Mexico,* Thomas Belt's *Naturalist in Nicaragua,* Adolph Bandelier's *The Gilded Man,* Bernal Diaz's *Conquest of Mexico,* Humboldt's *Vues des Cordillères,* and several volumes of the *Anales del Museo Nacional* of Mexico.[82] Though these books on New World antiquities show his interest in the past and the character of his reading, they account but little more than do the works of Frazer or Tylor for his knowledge of Quetzalcoatl. Lawrence's visits to the Aztec museum in Mexico City and to the pyramid at Teotihuacán were emotionally important no doubt.[83] But it was not until I consulted the Curator of Mexican Archaeology at the American Museum of Natural History, Dr. George Vaillant, that I discovered Lawrence's principal source. Dr. Vaillant informed me of something not yet in print, that Lawrence stayed for a time with the late Zelia

---

where there is no dancing. She has also said that the sacrificial cave in "The Woman Who Rode Away" is an actual cave near Taos (pp. 209–10, 213–14, 252).

[82] *Phoenix,* pp. 336, 355, 357, 359; *Mornings in Mexico,* pp. 93, 103; *Fantasia,* p. 8; *Plumed Serpent,* pp. 144, 343–44.

[83] *Letters,* pp. 565, 735; Frieda Lawrence, *"Not I, but the Wind . . . ,"* pp. 138, 140; *Plumed Serpent,* pp. 38–39, 62, 84–85.

Nuttall, the archaeologist, whose home near Mexico City contained a complete library of Mexicana. Here Lawrence's imagination found material to expand and room to digress. To express his gratitude Lawrence portrayed Mrs. Nuttall in *The Plumed Serpent* as the eccentric Mrs. Norris.[84] Depicting a host in such unflattering light might be considered a breach of decency on the part of another, but on the part of Lawrence it cannot be so construed; for she was a scientist and he could not abide a scientist. Furthermore, it was his custom to immortalize his friends and acquaintances.[85] Though Mrs. Norris is Mrs. Nuttall and Mrs. Nuttall's library is apparently responsible for much of Lawrence's learning, our knowledge of his relationship with its owner had been limited to the odd and perhaps insignificant detail, revealed in a letter, that during October, 1924, he bought her a doorknob.[86]

His debt to Mrs. Nuttall was not confined to the books by others in her library. From Mrs. Lawrence I learned that her husband read Mrs. Nuttall's *Fundamental Principles of Old and New World Civilizations*, 1901. To this formidable work Lawrence owed most of his wide but inaccurate knowledge of primitive Mexico. Mrs. Nuttall's theme is the ancient cult of the above and the below, the sky and the earth, embodied in two gods Huitzilopochtli and Tezcatlipoca; in Quetzalcoatl, the

[84] *Plumed Serpent*, pp. 34, 41.
[85] A prominent Indian general, for example, and the widow of a famous Harvard radical are said by Dr. Vaillant to appear in this novel as Don Cipriano and Kate.
[86] *Letters*, pp. 619, 620.

divine twin who symbolized the life-giving union of the two; and in two earthly rulers, the living representatives of the gods. Quetzalcoatl's name, meaning bird-serpent and twin, indicates duality, the bird standing for the above, the snake for the below, and twin for their union. He was the god of the fertilizing contact of wind and rain with fire and earth. Mrs. Nuttall's theory pleased Lawrence by its resemblance to animism and to polarity with sun and earth, and it gave him the device of the two gods and their earthly representatives for *The Plumed Serpent*. He modified her plan by suppressing Tezcatlipoca and by making Huitzilopochtli the god of earth, fire, and the below; but he allowed Quetzalcoatl to remain god of wind, rain, the above, and at the same time the supreme god of the union of rain with earth. Assisted perhaps by Frazer,[87] Lawrence adopted for his chapters "The First Waters" and "The First Rain" Mrs. Nuttall's idea of the rainy season as the time of the union of above and below, the time of fertility and spiritual rebirth. Kate's marriage to Don Cipriano in the rain is a symbolic treatment of this marriage of water and earth.

Much of the incidental symbolism, troubling no doubt to readers of *The Plumed Serpent*—the wheel, the eye, the eight-rayed black sun, the colors of the four cardinal points and of the gods—with allowance for Lawrence's carelessness may also be traced to Mrs. Nuttall. The morning star, another symbol of duality, associated with Quetzalcoatl in Aztec legend, is mentioned by Mrs.

[87] Quetzalcoatl was no doubt partly inspired by Frazer's dying and reborn god. See *The Plumed Serpent*, pp. 62–63. Cf. *Apocalypse* on dying and reborn gods.

Nuttall, but as inferior to Polaris.[88] For her Polaris, Lawrence wisely substituted Venus.

He did not get his knowledge of the Mexican gods entirely from his friend's book. Mrs. Nuttall does not mention the goddess Itzpapalotl, with whom Lawrence was going to identify the heroine of *The Plumed Serpent* until, halfway through the book, he forgot his purpose and chose another name for her. Neither does Mrs. Nuttall mention the dirt-eating goddess of love, mother of an obsidian knife, discussed by Lawrence in *Mornings in Mexico*.[89] It is probable that he read Lewis Spence's *Gods of Mexico,* 1923, the most convenient treatment of these two divinities. This likelihood is increased by the presence in Spence's book of Aztec hymns so close in character to those in *The Plumed Serpent* as to appear to have suggested their use to Lawrence.

He was not near Mrs. Nuttall's library when he wrote *The Plumed Serpent*. His dependence upon an imperfect memory accounts for one goddess of this book, a certain Malintzi, who is not in the Aztec pantheon. She seems to be the result of a casual union in Lawrence's fancy between two persons mentioned by Prescott, Metzli the moon and Malinche the mistress of Cortes.

Not Susan, still less these improvements to the Aztec pantheon, could detain the wanderer. Not even the primitive Utopia of Quetzalcoatl could quiet his disgust with the actual. On his way to Europe in the fall of 1925, he commenced a novel, *The Flying Fish,* never to be

[88] See *Phoenix*, p. 727, for Polaris. See *Apocalypse*, p. 163, for duality of the morning star.

[89] Pages 53–55.

completed, in which the ancient symbol of the fish is used to represent at once the decay of man from primitive excellence and the hope of return. From the ocean, the Greater Day of the ancients, the fish emerged to fly in the lesser day of the white men, but the laws of nature promised his descent. Aztecs, Mayas, and Zapotecs like the symbolical fish had once sported in the waters of the past. Although hoisted from the deep by the wretched men of Spain, the fishlike Indians preserved on their scales or in their blood some exemplary dew. That such dew could revive the wilted white is suggested in another Utopian work, the misnamed "Autobiographical Fragment," 1927, in which Lawrence entered the domain of H. G. Wells. Waking from a trance in the year 2927, Lawrence found the primitive society of his dreams in Nottingham. The mines, the wheels, the stacks, the heaps of slag had vanished, and in their place vegetarians danced Indian dances. These happy, instinctive men were like Egyptians. Lawrence was pleased.[90]

Once more in Italy, while the future impended and Susan ruminated in New Mexico, Lawrence turned his attention to the past. This time it was the Etruscans, about whom nobody knew very much, so that Lawrence's imagination was more than ordinarily unimpeded by fact. But preferring as usual to stray from what science could suggest, he looked into Mommsen's history, George Dennis's *Cities and Cemeteries of Etruria,* 1848, Fritz Weege's *Etruskische Malerei,* 1921, and several Italian studies; during 1926 and 1927 he visited the Etruscan Museum at Florence and the Etruscan tombs,

[90] *Phoenix,* pp. 825–32.

in company with his friend Earl Brewster.[91] Long before
this he had read about the Etruscan commerce with Atlantis in Frobenius's *Voice of Africa,* and he had shown
interest in the men of Etruria as early as 1921.[92] It
seemed to him that these remote people must have
known that polarity with nature which Quetzalcoatl had
served to symbolize. *Etruscan Places,* written in 1927, is
less a travel book than the editor of *Travel,* who published it serially, appears to have thought. Lawrence intended that these essays on the ram and bull-worshiping,
the dancing, Etruscans afford still another example to
the modern world. He found sermons in such urns, walls,
and symbols as survived, and he bitterly blamed the
Romans whose aqueducts and sewers had removed all
other traces of ancient virtue.

While blaming the Romans in the spring of 1927, he
wrote "The Man Who Died," [93] a story of Jesus. In this
work Lawrence played with a conceit which had occupied Samuel Butler and George Moore. But although
Lawrence's Saviour also escaped death on the cross, He
differs from His predecessors. By a priestess of Isis, who
confuses Him with Osiris, the Laurentian Jesus is con-

[91] *Etruscan Places,* pp. 123, 128; Frieda Lawrence, *"Not I, but the
Wind . . . ,"* pp. 208, 225; Ada Lawrence and G. S. Gelder, *Early Life,*
p. 108; Brewster, *Reminiscences,* pp. 99, 117, 122, 128, 137; *Letters,*
pp. 659, 680, 682. Mohr sent Lawrence a book on the Etruscans in
November, 1929: "Letters of Lawrence to Max Mohr," *T'ien Hsia
Monthly,* I (September, 1935), p. 175.

[92] *Letters,* p. 527. In 1928 he was to order from a bookseller David
Randall-MacIver's *Iron Age in Italy* and to read *Downland Man* by
H. J. Massingham, who wrote on birds, Shelley, and pre-Roman
Britain: *Letters,* p. 704. Lawrence's poem "Cypresses" celebrates the
Etruscans, *Collected Poems,* II, 147. Cf. his other primitivistic poems,
"Almond Blossom" and "Sicilian Cyclamens," *ibid.,* pp. 159, 166.

[93] Brewster, *Reminiscences,* p. 128.

verted to the theory of polarity. Lawrence was far from liberal. He could not tolerate the slightest deviation from the heterodox.

From Jesus he turned his attention to the Book of Revelation in which, beneath the Christian surface, he saw some vestiges of the old worship of nature. The stars, dragons, horses, colors, numbers were symbols common to the early Greeks, the Etruscans, Chaldeans, Egyptians, and Hindus. These intuitive men had lived religiously breast to breast with sun, beast, and tree, before the later Greeks, the Romans, and the Christians, with their mechanical ideals, came between man and nature. Pursuing his symbols, finding the Woman to have been the Great Mother, the Witnesses to represent the heavenly twins, and the Beast and his number to mean polarity, Lawrence confessed his nostalgia for the ancient world and prayed the lovely green dragon to lead man back to his roots for a new start.[94]

Like his other works on the ancients, *Apocalypse* owes much to Lawrence's reading. I have shown the sources upon which Lawrence drew for his Egyptian, Mexican, and Etruscan wanderings; and in the next chapter I shall discuss the major sources of *Apocalypse*. Here I shall mention two of the minor ones, the psychoanalytical and the Greek.

Just after the war Lawrence appears to have read Jung's *Psychology of the Unconscious*,[95] a work which shows the myths and symbols of primitive man to be

94 *Apocalypse*, pp. 40–41, 50, 143, 152, 159–60, 162, 173, 182, 200.
95 See *supra*, p. 98.

resident in the unconscious of modern man. This theory seems to have appealed to Lawrence as suggesting a way of return to the past through the resident symbol. In his Mexican writings he referred to "the memories of old, far-off, far, far-off experience that lie within us" [96] and to primitive symbols which, though neglected by the conscious mind, are embedded in the soul. No doubt this idea had much to do with Lawrence's interest in the myth and symbols of Quetzalcoatl; and *Apocalypse* is plainly a study of the primitive baggage in man's unconscious, of the dragon now deep in our minds, of the horse, which still "roams the dark underworld meadows of the soul." [97] Such internal vestiges of glory, conveniently objectified by St. John, gave Lawrence more hope of restoration than all the pots of Etruria.

Of the early Greeks, who were as good as the Etruscans and as amorous of duality as Quetzalcoatl himself, Lawrence had much to say in *Apocalypse*. He refers learnedly to Anaximander, Empedokles, Pythagoras, Xenophanes, and Anaximenes, to their theories of the four elements, and to Herakleitos, from whom he quotes. It was this quotation that enabled me to identify the source of his learning as John Burnet's *Early Greek Philosophy*.[98] From Burnet's version of the remains of Herakleitos, Lawrence quotes (with quotation marks) Fragment 30 and (without quotation marks) portions of Fragments

[96] *Phoenix*, pp. 99, 296, 301, 759.
[97] *Apocalypse*, pp. 97, 100, 126, 142, 144, 173.
[98] Published 1892; reprinted 1908 and 1920. I am using the 1920 edition (London, Black). This work is the most convenient treatment in English of Anaximander, Anaximenes, Pythagoras, Xenophanes, Herakleitos, Empedokles, and Anaxagoras.

22 and 32, which he combines and makes his own.[99] He closely paraphrases Burnet's commentary several times and, except for some careless departures, follows his author in the matter of the balance and strife of the elements.[100] It is plain that he had this book before him when he wrote. It is likely, moreover, that Burnet's work, which provided so much for *Apocalypse,* was also the source of Lawrence's earlier knowledge of the Greeks and one of the principal ingredients of the theory of polarity.[101] While he was writing *Apocalypse,*[102] Lawrence also read Gilbert Murray's *Five Stages of Greek Religion,* but apart from some passages on pre-Hellenic *Urdummheit* and on the worship of bulls, cows, and snakes, about which he already knew, this book seems not to have had much in it for him. He read and disagreed with the Venerable Robert Henry Charles's commentary on Revelation,[103] and he used Hastings's *Encyclopedia of Religion and Ethics,*[104] in which he could have come upon many useful things.

While his fancy, like the symbolical horse, roamed the forests of the past, his body was forced to content itself with the Italian peasants. He now expected little

[99] Burnet translates the fragments of Herakleitos. Cf. *Apocalypse,* pp. 160–61, with Burnet, pp. 97 and 135.

[100] Cf. *Apocalypse,* pp. 56–57, 76, 159, 160–61, 167, 168, with Burnet, pp. 8, 9, 53–54, 57, 66–68, 73, 81, 109, 122, 123, 137, 143, 145, 153, 163, 166, 197, 209, 228, 232, 238, 296–97. See also *Last Poems,* pp. 36, 41.

[101] The theory of polarity is based in part, as we have seen, on the ancient Greek ideas of duality, equilibrium, and the balance and strife of opposite elements. Burnet is the most likely source.

[102] Brewster, *Reminiscences,* p. 305.

[103] *Apocalypse,* pp. 58, 61, 69. Besides *A Critical and Exegetical Commentary on the Revelation of St. John* (Edinburgh, Clark, 1920), Dr. Charles wrote other commentaries on this book of the Bible, and in 1920 he published an edition of it.

[104] *Apocalypse,* p. 70.

of them, but their vital presence gave him what comfort
he could find.[105] As he listened to their bucolic cries and
tramplings, his thoughts, still Minoan, returned to the
American shore. He dreamed of going out to see "if
Susan, the black cow, has gone to her nest among the
trees, for the night. Cows don't eat much at night. But
Susan will wander in the moon." [106]

[105] *Assorted Articles,* p. 153.
[106] *Mornings in Mexico,* pp. 186–87.

CHAPTER FIVE

SUSAN UNVEILED

SUSAN might wander in the moon or, as cows will, jump over it, yet the meaning of her conduct would escape all but children or adepts. To the latter, especially to theosophists, cow and moon and their almost unspeakable connection are known; for the wisdom of the East, handed down from Atlantis and preserved by Hindus, Chaldeans, Egyptians, and Mme Blavatsky, has unveiled the theosophical eye, that third or pineal eye by which the truth is perceived. Through this eye William Butler Yeats contemplated cats and the eight-and-twenty phases of the moon; Dr. Anna Kingsford, standing before tall windows in her oriental shift, welcomed the moon at its full; and D. H. Lawrence saw Susan plain in the loony night. His moonings may be traced to his passion not only for the mindless and the primitive but for the oriental and the occult. To the other ingredients of his developing religion he added theosophy, yoga, and astrology.

For two hundred years before the time of Lawrence, emotional men of the West, impatient of the tedium of civilization and discontented with the here and now, had turned to the Orient. In the eighteenth century, some, to be sure, faced eastward because they found in Confucius or in an imaginary Abyssinian, Persian, or Chinese philosopher signs of a civilization superior in many ways to their own and devices for the correction of follies. Of this sort were Voltaire, Montesquieu, Goldsmith, and

Dr. Johnson. Many men of this time, however, found in the East not a more reasonable way of life but the exotic, the mysterious, and the remote. To such men, thoughts of the East brought that holiday from reason and order which the noble savage and the Gothic castle brought to their contemporaries. As Joseph Warton roamed the forests of his fancy in America, and as Walpole took his pleasure in Strawberry Hill, English gardeners were plotting Chinese gardens to relieve the regularity of Versailles. Makers of furniture, who found the most restless rococo inadequate, constructed Chinese cabinets and chairs. Thomas Taylor, the Platonist, was said to have stained his back parlor with the blood of goatish sacrifice as he pondered the mysteries of Eleusis or the doctrines of Chaldea and of Hermes Trismegistus. William Blake was fascinated with the *Bhagavadgita* as well as with Boehme and Swedenborg. Indeed, the fashion of the oriental and the strange became so strong that it moved many who had no quarrel with civilization. Even the most elegant composer in the world wrote Turkish music.

During the nineteenth century, English poets found emotional relief in Xanadu, Kehama, the Light of Asia, or the wisdom of the Sufis. But in the transcendentalism of America the appeal of the East is more apparent. Emerson and Thoreau, rejecting the rationalism of the eighteenth century and impatient of Christianity, however unreasonable Christianity might appear, discovered what they wanted in Hinduism, Buddhism, and other eastern systems. Emerson's Oversoul owes no more to German metaphysics than to the

Vedas, the *Upanishads,* and the *Bhagavadgita,* for example, and to Confucius, who, however reasonable he might appear, had the advantage of being remote in place and time. Thoreau called himself a yogi, and, as far as his knowledge of Hinduism, his character, and the climate of Walden permitted, he was one. The orientalists of Concord took from the East what they found suited to their purposes, combining it with what they had, so that, as Dr. Arthur Christy says,[1] they produced eclectic syntheses of eastern, German, and Yankee elements. A dogmatic Hindu might quarrel with their mixture of alien matters, but the ideas of Emerson and Thoreau remained oriental enough to satisfy all but the captious and to provide for themselves the distraction they needed. Two hundred years earlier, Sir Thomas Browne, the follower of Bacon, had loved to confound and recreate his understanding with enigmas. "I love to lose myself in a mystery," he said, "to pursue my Reason to an *O altitudo!*" By the middle of the nineteenth century, after an age of matter and reason, Sir Thomas's recreation had become Emerson's necessity.

The increase in materialism after Darwin called for even more spiritual measures. In response, Mme Blavatsky emerged, coming to New York in 1875 from Thibet, she said, to found the Theosophical Society. Assisted by Colonel H. S. Olcott, she began to advance the cause of the spirit by spreading information about oriental philosophies, by invoking occult powers, and

[1] *The Orient in American Transcendentalism* (New York, Columbia University Press, 1932). I owe much to my conversations with my colleague Dr. Christy, who is one of the principal authorities on the relations between East and West.

by assuring the sensitive that nature is not blind and mechanical. As apostle to the materialists of the West she issued *Isis Unveiled*, 1877, and *The Secret Doctrine*, 1888, long, disorderly, and, to the uninitiate, tedious collections of oriental and occult wisdom, which served her followers as scriptures. Theosophy, she announced, had undertaken the role which Christianity had been unable to support and, supplanting the decorous, the feeble, and the ignorant, now came forward as leader in the "titanic struggle between materialism and spiritual aspirations." She lost no time in abusing Huxley, Tyndall, Spencer, Comte, Faraday, and the Pope and in return suffered much abuse; but as she said of herself, with one of her quieter moments perhaps in mind, "at slander she smiles in silent contempt."

To those whose emotions had been starved by Darwin, cities, and factories, who found themselves unable, after Darwin, to return to their childhood faith, she offered spiritual release in that body of secret wisdom which she had been able to recapture by the aid of certain eastern adepts and by her own synthesis of occult, oriental, and early beliefs. All spiritual systems of the past, she said, point to one ancient truth, whence they came. The central element of this ancient wisdom—or theosophy, as it is now known, which surpasses as it includes and explains all other occult doctrines—is metempsychosis, the evolution of individuals under the law of Karma from spirit to matter and back again seven times in seven planes around a chain of seven planets, of which this earth in this plane alone is visible. In the present cycle on this earth, primitive man was more spiritual than the modern scientist, who is at the lowest material point of development, limited to reason and unable to know the truth by intuition and instinct. Without this useful capacity, which primitive man and Mme Blavatsky enjoyed, Huxley, for example, found it impossible to follow them in their contemplation of the various orders of spirits, such as fairies, salamanders, and vampires, of the meaning of sun, moon, cow, serpent, and lotus, of the mysteries of alchemy, astrology, yoga, and numerology, and of the beauty of Isis, from whom Mme Blavatsky had just removed the veil.

Isis had been nude before the Flood. In this happy time, the men of Atlantis, who supported a priesthood even more knowing than themselves, though they themselves intuitively possessed a science far riper than Darwin's, had been privileged to examine her. But later —and this was the Fall of Man—their descendants degenerated into materialism, and a veil at first impaired, then all but hid, her beauty. In a sense, remarked Mme Blavatsky, the Darwinists were right about evolution, but what they took to be the ascent of man from the ape was the descent of man from Atlantean perfection to the state of ape, cave man, and scientist. Even after the passing of Atlantis and the degeneration of man, however, the ancient wisdom, although corrupted, dispersed, and incompletely understood, was handed down by archaic peoples like the Egyptians, the Hindus, the Chaldeans, the Druids, and the Aztecs, and by adepts, who were all but all-knowing, such as Hermes Trismegistus, Pythagoras, Herakleitos, Paracelsus, the Kabalists, the Rosicrucians, the Mahatmas of Thibet, and Mme Blavatsky.

According to the state of the times and to the facilities at their disposal these men, as wise as serpents, celebrated the truth in the Eleusinian mysteries or in the New York Lodge of the Theosophical Society. They and their disciples could discover the secret doctrine veiled beneath the myths and symbols of the great religions, in the Bible and the *Vedas,* for instance, or the inscriptions on Aztec and Egyptian monuments. However fragmentary, however misunderstood by sectaries and archaeologists, these symbolic vestiges correspond to truths recorded in Anima Mundi, in which all is recorded. Such symbols are the keys by which the theosophist may open the gates of Atlantis and come face to face with what's what.

A doctrine which promised the spiritual, the remote, and the profound to those who were looking for them pleased many Americans and more Englishmen. During the eighties Anna Kingsford and A. P. Sinnett made the secret doctrine less secret in the London Lodge. By the time of Mme Blavatsky's arrival in England in 1887, her English disciples, whose books rivaled her own in popularity, were bringing comfort to hundreds who had drooped at the name of Huxley. Of these, Annie Besant was the most eminent. This extraordinary woman, who had abandoned husband, home, and religion, had become an atheist, an evolutionist, a socialist, a friend of Bernard Shaw's, and, what is worse, a Neo-Malthusian. But years spent in support of Bradlaugh, Huxley, and Sidney Webb had left her without spiritual satisfaction. Descending from the soapbox in Hyde Park which she had shared for years with other Fabian orators, she looked about her and paused to consider the plight of this restless and eager generation—surrounded by forces we dimly see but cannot as yet understand, discontented with old ideas and half afraid of new, greedy for the material results of the knowledge brought us by Science but looking askance at her agnosticism as regards the soul, fearful of superstition but still more fearful of atheism, turning from the husks of out-grown creeds but filled with desperate hunger for spiritual ideals . . .[2]

At this crisis, in her capacity of reviewer for a materialistic magazine, she came upon the works of Sinnett and Mme Blavatsky and, saved from materialism, entered the household of the latter, to become after her death her successor. Unable immediately to discard rhetoric and logic, Mrs. Besant wrote many books in the effort to make clear what had been at once announced and confused in the writings of Mme Blavatsky.

Men of letters, more gifted than Mrs. Besant but no less impatient with the times, found similar refuge in theosophy. William Butler Yeats said—and the repetition of what he said will do no harm, for it is important— "I am very religious, and deprived by Huxley and Tyndall, whom I detested, of the simple-minded religion of my childhood, I . . . made a new religion, almost an infallible church of poetic tradition . . ."[3] By poetic tradition he meant not only that but also theosophy. Saved from the spiritual Waste Land in 1885 by his discovery of A. P. Sinnett, Yeats and his friends Charles Johnston and A.E. founded a "household" of hermetic students, which was chartered in 1886 as the Dublin Lodge of the Theosophical Society. Here they read the *Upanishads* and the works of Mme Blavatsky, experi-

[2] Preface, *An Autobiography* (Philadelphia, Altemus, 1893).
[3] *Autobiographies* (New York, Macmillan, 1927), p. 142.

mented with ceremonial magic, repeated the yoga aphorisms of Patanjali, heard lectures by Colonel Olcott, Mrs.
Besant, and visiting Hindus, and spiritually dined on
vegetables. In 1889 Yeats visited Mme Blavatsky in London and was permitted by her to smell spectral incense
and to hear astral bells. These were comforting but less
important to a poet than her ideas about myths and
symbols. He found from her writings that symbols have
power by occult correspondence to bridge the gap between matter and Anima Mundi. In search of such magical devices he studied the works of Boehme, Swedenborg,
Blake, and Liddle MacGregor Mathers, the Kabalist. He
knew what Mme Blavatsky never tired of saying, that the
myths and symbols of all lands are keys to the same reality, and, after some Kabalistical experiments, he returned to the more convenient symbols and legends of
his own people. The Irish hounds, trees, fish, deer, and
roses of his early poems and the poems themselves are of
mysterious import; for the spiritual poet had learned
from Mme Blavatsky that an Irish poem could be an
occult instrument, the Irish poet a magician. Though
the years gave him sense and improved his poetry, he
still continued to delight in the occult, in mediums, and
in the phases of the moon. To Yeats the occult was not
only what his spirit but what his art required. As some
poets of the nineties found in alcohol or splendid sins
that excitement which earlier poets had found in more
respectable traditions, so Yeats, still religiously inclined,
found his stimulation in the deep and the remote.

He knew what he was about, but his friend A.E. was
an innocent theosophist, less poet than mystic. Without

the interference of reason, he accepted the teachings of
initiates and, abandoning himself to the oriental trance,
wrote his verses to the dictation of spirits. If the result
had been better, his confidence in Mme Blavatsky would
appear to have been less misplaced. But thanks to her
his life was not uninteresting; nor can it seem wanting
in value to the historian of the late nineteenth century.
A.E. is the most extreme example of a tendency, num-
bering many in France as well as in the British Isles, of
which Huysmans in *Là-bas* and Yeats in "Rosa Alchemica" gave some account. Telling in melodious prose of
orgies among alembics, of ceremonies with elementals
on the hermetic floor, of spiritual alchemy and much
else, "Rosa Alchemica" is the symbolic history of a generation. In England, Arthur Machen was deep in esoteric, even diabolical, mysteries. In France, where the
Black Mass and the Christian Kabala afforded some relief from Zola and Pasteur, the so-called symbolist movement carried many to, and sometimes across, the borders
of the ineffable. Arthur Rimbaud, a reader of Eliphas
Lévi, dabbled in the occult. Villiers de l'Isle-Adam rev-
eled in magical symbols, and Maeterlinck owed no little
of his uncertainty to oriental mysticism. When Yeats
visited France in the nineties to meet Eliphas Lévi and
Stanislaus de Guaita and to experiment in a more suitable atmosphere with Kabalistical numerology, he found
Strindberg lost in identical distractions.

By the time of Lawrence, the occult and oriental response to materialism had been fixed by the impact of
similar conditions upon equally spiritual temperaments.
Lawrence was familiar with Emerson, Thoreau, Blake,

and Maeterlinck, and, however great his ignorance of Yeats and A.E. may have been, his temper was much the same as theirs, the growing materialism of the times even less agreeable to such a temper. His reaction, like theirs, naturally took the form of anti-intellectualism, hatred of science, primitivism, and reliance upon intuition. When he came upon the works of Mme Blavatsky, whose response to the times had anticipated his own in so many ways, he also found her congenial. Pleased by her support and instructed by her learning, he became confirmed in what he had already felt and, taking from her the oriental and the occult, added them to his private religion.

In a letter of 1919 to a friend who was evidently in spiritual distress, Lawrence recommended Mme Blavatsky's *Isis Unveiled,* and, although its exact title at the time escaped him, he especially recommended her *Secret Doctrine.*[4] He did not own these big expensive works, he said, but had read copies borrowed from friends. Although, according to his habit, he qualified his praise of what he had found useful, saying that Mme Blavatsky's books, while good, were "not *very* much good," Mrs. Lawrence has informed me that her husband read and delighted in all of Mme Blavatsky's works and that, as he read, he used to smile at the "mundane egg," an occult object of which, judging by the number of allusions to it in their works, neither Mme Blavatsky nor Lawrence ever tired.[5] The first of these allusions in his work, occurring in "The Crown," 1915, points to the

[4] *Letters,* p. 476.
[5] For example, *Porcupine,* pp. 134–35; *Phoenix,* p. 743.

period between 1912 and 1915 as the time of his first encounter with the secret doctrine.[6] He also alludes several times to Annie Besant, sometimes unfavorably, once as one of the few leaders left.[7] Mrs. Lawrence has told me that he read many of Mrs. Besant's works as well as several by Rudolph Steiner, the German theosophist.[8]

Although Lawrence could sneer at certain "herb-eating occultists" whom he met in 1917 in Cornwall,[9] he confessed during the same year that nothing but "deep subjects" interested him, and, during the next year, he admitted reading "another book on *Occultism*," dealing with magic and astrology, which he found "very interesting, and important—though antipathetic" to him. "Certainly magic is a reality," he proceeded, "—not by any means the nonsense Bertie Russell says it is." [10] However antipathetic the occult might have been to him, Lawrence was also a reader of *The Occult Review*, which he recommended together with Mme Blavatsky to his friend in distress.[11] This periodical was published by Rider, whose shop Lawrence suggested as the place above all others for procuring transcendental literature.[12] As every theosophist knows, Rider is still in busi-

[6] *Porcupine*, pp. 62–63. Lawrence's poem "Don Juan" (published in *Poetry*, December, 1914) contains allusions to the mystery of Isis and the beloved seven; and "Rose of All the World," a poem written as early as 1912, mentions "The Great Breath."

[7] *Letters*, p. 705; *Fantasia*, p. 16; *Porcupine*, p. 120; *Tales*, p. 1016.

[8] In his book on Lawrence, M. Seillière has conjectured without evidence that Lawrence knew the work of Steiner; but M. Seillière's ignorance of theosophy prevented him from drawing the proper conclusions from his improper assumption.

[9] *Letters*, p. 415.   [10] *Ibid.*, p. 440.

[11] Lewis Spence, whose book on the Aztec gods Lawrence probably read, wrote for this magazine.

[12] *Letters*, p. 476.

ness, publishing books on Atlantis and India, for example, and the Third Eye.

Allusions throughout Lawrence's essays show his familiarity with theosophical terms and fancies. His discussions of the symbolic lotus or lily, for example, reflect those of Mme Blavatsky.[13] The title of his essay "Him with His Tail in His Mouth" comes from the symbol of the tail-biting serpent by which theosophists suggest eternity, metempsychosis, and other matters.[14] His references to the thrice-greatest Hermes, the "mystic Om," and the "Sanskrit joys of Purusha, Pradhana, Kala," [15] to which Mme Blavatsky devotes much attention in *The Secret Doctrine,* are so casual as to suggest long acquaintance with theosophy.

The stories and novels he wrote before 1925 offer comparatively little indication of his occult interests. But Count Psanek, the dark primitivist of "The Ladybird," 1923, makes up for this neglect. This mindless Czechoslovakian is described as "an initiate" in an old esoteric society, possessing an "awful secret knowledge" about the nature of the real sun, about the affinity between moon and water, about Egypt and Isis, and about hermetic gold. His symbolic scarab is decorated with seven spots, and about the base of his symbolic thimble, also decorated with seven spots, is coiled a snake. Clearly the Count is a member of some central European lodge of the Theosophical Society.[16] In *St. Mawr,* 1925, the hero-

13 *Phoenix,* pp. 61–64, 218–19; *Porcupine,* pp. 75–76; *Women in Love,* p. 100.

14 Cf. an early reference to this theosophical symbol of eternity in "The Crown," *Porcupine,* p. 28.

15 *Porcupine,* pp. 127, 230; *Fantasia,* p. 16.

16 *Tales,* pp. 370, 372, 374, 378–79, 382, 390.

ine, instructed by the astrological and alchemical Mr. Cartwright, who appears to have consulted *The Secret Doctrine*, feels that her Third Eye is opening.[17] The hero of *Kangaroo* knows about Hermes Trismegistus, but otherwise he would fail to interest a theosophist.

Not all of Lawrence's occult references imply favor, nor is his tone without some condescension on the several occasions when he mentions theosophy directly. "Even theosophists," he remarked, "don't realize that the universal lotus really blossoms in the abdomen . . ."[18] The manifest unfairness of this remark suggests what acquaintance with Lawrence's nature makes certain, that his knowledge of this as of other subjects remained incomplete and that it would be improper to call him an orthodox theosophist. The best of eastern thought is eternal, he said, but, he added, he was not one for taking it "wholesale."[19] Like Emerson, he took from the Orient what he found useful, ignoring or rejecting the rest. During certain of his attacks upon scientific evolution, for example, he maintained, like Mme Blavatsky, that life unfolds in cycles, and he alluded once to shedding avatars and recovering an earlier self, but metempsychosis, however important it might be to the orthodox, seems not to have captured his fancy.[20] What is hardly less irregular, he condemned Anima Mundi as an abstraction;[21] and although Mme

[17] *Ibid.*, pp. 598, 600–601.

[18] *Psychoanalysis*, p. 92; cf. *Porcupine*, p. 120, and *Tales*, p. 1018.

[19] Brewster, *Reminiscences*, pp. 104–5.

[20] *Fantasia*, p. 10; *Letters*, pp. 412, 498; *Porcupine*, pp. 216, 239; *Mornings in Mexico*, pp. 9–14; *Assorted Articles*, pp. 46–48; *Tales*, p. 879; *Apocalypse*, p. 148.

[21] *Phoenix*, p. 708.

Blavatsky had approved of Buddhism, and Lawrence's friend Earl Brewster was a New England Buddhist, Lawrence made the same objection to the Oversoul, Karma, Nirvana,[22] and the other conceits of the Buddhists. Such notions were too mental, too egoistic, too recent, or too peaceful, he felt, to fit into his philosophy.

In a short story called "Things," written late in his career, he caricatured two New England idealists who had fled from the materialism of their country to Buddha and Mrs. Besant. These ignoble fugitives were probably intended by their friend as portraits of Mr. and Mrs. Brewster, to whom he had been indebted for many kindnesses and whose notions and behavior were not as alien to his own as he chose to pretend. After his own flight from the materialism of England and while under the spell of Mr. Brewster, Lawrence had suspended his hostility to Buddhism and had looked to a bo tree in Ceylon with some hope, but his visit to the East, undertaken in part with such hope, had left him longing for the West. Later he still wanted that compromise between East and West for which Mr. Brewster was working, but this time, disenchanted by Ceylon, Lawrence suggested the pre-Buddhistic as the eastern element of the confusion.[23]

In view of his usual opinion of Buddha, it was natural for him to reject the Oversoul of Emerson, Thoreau, and Whitman as equally mechanical and ideal. Their

[22] But note his acceptance of Nirvana in *Last Poems*, pp. 68–75.

[23] Brewster, *Reminiscences*, pp. 20, 43, 45, 96, 98, 108; Luhan, *Lorenzo in Taos*, pp. 15, 18, 19, 151; *Letters*, pp. 534, 542, 543, 546; *Apocalypse*, p. 74; *Psychoanalysis*, p. 36; *Mornings in Mexico*, p. 101; *Porcupine*, p. 185; *Phoenix*, pp. 204 ff., 662; *Aaron's Rod*, p. 122.

"mundane egg of oneness" seemed to him to be inimical to individuality or, on another occasion, to be too individualistic.[24] He had learned much from Emerson and Thoreau, but doctrinal differences had arisen between masters and pupil. These differences, however, do not account for the vehemence of his denial, which is explained rather by his quickness to deny predecessors or rivals who appeared to impair his sense of his own originality. For his personal emblem he had chosen the Phoenix, and the Phoenix, as everybody knows, has neither father nor uncles. Not everybody knows, however, that according to Mme Blavatsky in *The Secret Doctrine*,[25] the lonely, self-begetting Phoenix is an esoteric symbol of initiation and rebirth. Her discussion of this singular bird makes it seem possible that Lawrence's Phoenix had a mother or, at least, an aunt.

Purusha, the lotus, the initiation of Count Psanek, an awareness of Hermes, snakes, and the number seven, and a not impossible Phoenix may seem—and, indeed, are—trivial spoils for even an eclectic theosophist to carry away with him from the secret doctrine. These matters are decorations, significant as evidence of occult interests, not otherwise important. But although Mme Blavatsky had been unable to secure his acceptance of Buddha, Anima Mundi, metempsychosis, and other vital matters, she gave Lawrence two important ideas, which affected several of his later works: the idea of the primitive religious Utopia and the idea of ancient

[24] *Phoenix*, pp. 24, 188, 190, 705, 713, 740, 741–44, 763.
[25] Los Angeles, Theosophy Co., 1925, II, 617.

myths and symbols as the way of understanding and return.

When he forgot its symbolic meaning,[26] Lawrence regarded the ocean as an ugly, grey cemetery "where the bright, lost world of Atlantis is buried"; [27] and, like Mme Blavatsky, he said: "I believe that there was a great age, a great epoch . . . previous to 2000 B. C." [28] He shared her opinion that the cave man was a degenerate survivor of this Utopian epoch [29] and her opinion that the American Indian preserves in his ceremonies "a living tradition going back far beyond the birth of Christ, beyond the pyramids, beyond Moses. A vast old religion which once swayed the earth," he said, "lingers in unbroken practice there in New Mexico . . ." [30] In the voice of the Indian, reciting the legends of his people, both Lawrence and Mme Blavatsky heard echoes from "away back . . . before the Flood." [31] The theosophical pursuit of the antediluvian explains not only much of Lawrence's interest in the redskin but also much of his concern with the Egyptians, Chaldeans, Etruscans, and other ancient people, in whom Mme Blavatsky had detected traces of better days.

In the preceding chapter, Lawrence's interest in the world of the Aztec and the Egyptian was described as primitivistic. It should be apparent now that his prim-

[26] In *The Flying Fish*, an unfinished novel published in *Phoenix*, he also uses the ocean theosophically as a symbol of the spiritual world and the fish as a symbol of the spiritual man.

[27] *Phoenix*, p. 797.

[28] *Ibid.*, p. 769; cf. *Apocalypse*, pp. 73–74.

[29] *Tales*, p. 596; *Phoenix*, pp. 298–99.

[30] *Phoenix*, p. 145.   [31] *Ibid.*, p. 146.

itivism was at least partly theosophical in origin and
character. His interest in the past was nearer that of
Mme Blavatsky than that of the common primitivist.
Both he and she read archaeologists and anthropologists
for information, and both displayed the same contempt
of the scientists by whom they were informed. What in
their materialism the archaeologists were unable to understand, as they blindly dug and patiently uncovered
the relics of the past, Mme Blavatsky was able to understand through intuition and the teachings of her Mahatmas. Lawrence knew more than the archaeologists,
through intuition and the teachings of Mme Blavatsky.
This inscrutable woman lurked in the offing when Lawrence said that he had found hints in all kinds of
scholarly books but that, although his soul was stimulated by the relics uncovered by the scientists, he proceeded by intuition.[32]

Concerning such symbols of the ancients as the cross,
the tree, the wheel, the snake, and the bull, his observations reveal the same guidance. To him, as to Mme
Blavatsky, the identical symbols of the Aztec and the
Egyptian were clues to the same religious past. When, in
Mornings in Mexico,[33] he compared the Indian with
the Egyptian and noted the symbols of snake and sun,
he was echoing his spiritual instructor. His soul also
throbbed at the thought of an Egyptian ankh, a device
which, with the annular serpent, decorates the cover of
The Secret Doctrine. The symbols of the Bible also led

[32] *Fantasia*, pp. 7, 10.

[33] Pages 153, 155, 159. See his poem "Tortoise Shell" (*Collected Poems*,
II, 224) in which he perceives the ancient symbols of cross and number
on the reptilian shell.

him to Chaldea and beyond. He said, as she had said before him, that the profound truths embedded in the symbolism of old religious documents carry the initiate "back in great cyclic swoops through eras of time." [34]

Such cyclic swoops lent interest to the series of articles on classic American literature which Lawrence contributed in 1918 and 1919 to that advanced periodical *The English Review*. When he came to publish these articles in a book, prudence or the advice of his publisher caused Lawrence to omit his references to ancient numerology, to the Eleusinian mysteries, to that union of religion and science which an esoteric priesthood once enjoyed, and to the times before the Flood when initiates and adepts of Atlantis understood the ankh, the circle, and the rosy cross. [35]

Symbolic clues to the past were never more knowingly followed by the most orthodox theosophist. [36] Lawrence's scattered remarks on symbolism, however, are less significant of his theosophical position than the Foreword to *Fantasia of the Unconscious*, 1922, a work described by him as an attempt "to stammer out the first terms of a forgotten knowledge." This preface, which is, perhaps, the most important passage for the understanding of his later work, might have been written by Mme Blavatsky herself:

[34] *Apocalypse*, p. 126; cf. pp. 42, 52, 61, 113, 184–85, and also *Fantasia*, p. 68; *Phoenix*, pp. 295–96, 303, 738; *Psychoanalysis*, p. 113.

[35] See, for example, "The Spirit of Place," *The English Review*, XXVII (November, 1918), 321. Cf. *ibid.*, XXVIII (February, 1919), 89; XXVIII (June, 1919), 477, 478, 479, 484, 485.

[36] In his poem "Grapes" (*Collected Poems*, II, 133) even the fruit of the vine serves as a symbol to carry him back to the pre-Flood world, where dark, pristine Atlanteans roamed.

I honestly think that the great pagan world of which Egypt and Greece were the last living terms, the great pagan world which preceded our own era once, had a vast and perhaps perfect science of its own, a science in terms of life. In our era this science crumbled into magic and charlatanry. But even wisdom crumbles.

I believe that this great science previous to ours and quite different in constitution and nature from our science once was universal, established all over the then-existing globe. I believe it was esoteric, invested in a large priesthood. Just as mathematics and mechanics and physics are defined and expounded in the same way in the universities of China or Bolivia or London or Moscow to-day, so, it seems to me, in the great world previous to ours a great science and cosmology were taught esoterically in all countries of the globe, Asia, Polynesia, America, Atlantis and Europe. Belt's suggestion [37] of the geographical nature of this previous world seems to me most interesting. In the period which geologists call the Glacial Period, the waters of the earth must have been gathered up in a vast body on the higher places of our globe, vast worlds of ice. And the sea-beds of to-day must have been comparatively dry. So that the Azores rose up mountainous from the plain of Atlantis, where the Atlantic now washes, and the Easter Isles and the Marquesas and the rest rose lofty from the marvellous great continent of the Pacific.

In that world men lived and taught and knew, and were in one complete correspondence over all the earth. Men wandered back and forth from Atlantis to the Polynesian Continent as men now sail from Europe to America. The interchange was complete, and knowledge, science was universal over the earth, cosmopolitan as it is to-day.

Then came the melting of the glaciers, and the world flood. The refugees from the drowned continents fled to the high places of America, Europe, Asia, and the Pacific Isles. And some degenerated naturally into cave men, neolithic and palæolithic creatures, and some retained their marvellous innate beauty and life-perfection, as the South Sea Is-

---

[37] He refers to Thomas Belt, *The Naturalist in Nicaragua*, Chapter XIV.

landers, and some wandered savage in Africa, and some, like Druids or Etruscans or Chaldeans or Amerindians or Chinese, refused to forget, but taught the old wisdom, only in its half-forgotten, symbolic forms. More or less forgotten, as knowledge: remembered as ritual, gesture, and myth-story.

And so, the intense potency of symbols is part at least memory. And so it is that all the great symbols and myths which dominate the world when our history first begins, are very much the same in every country and every people, the great myths all relate to one another. And so it is that these myths now begin to hypnotize us again, our own impulse towards our own scientific way of understanding being almost spent. And so, besides myths, we find the same mathematic figures, cosmic graphs which remain among the aboriginal peoples in all continents, mystic figures and signs whose true cosmic or scientific significance is lost, yet which continue in use for purposes of conjuring or divining.

If my reader finds this bosh and abracadabra, all right for him.

This is simple theosophy, but Lawrence was too eclectic and too much of an individualist to follow one guide all the way. Though he took from Mme Blavatsky his idea of a religious Utopia in the past, with an esoteric wisdom to which vestigial symbols are the clues, he did not accept her idea of the nature of this wisdom. Her Atlanteans believed in metempsychosis, a belief which did not appeal to Lawrence, who, with the aid of intuition and some additional reading, spurned the orthodox doctrine and, like his ancestor who had been displeased by some point of Anglican dogma, became a dissenter. His Atlanteans danced to a drum. The religion which once inspired the world and symbolically survived in Lawrence's Egypt or Mexico was primitive animism. His Utopia, which had its origin in Blavatsky, took its character from Frazer, Tylor, and Harrison; his

Atlantis owed something to the labors of Frobenius, Nuttall, and Belt. These materialists were corrected and made acceptable to Lawrence's religious nature by theosophy, and theosophy was brought up to date and made acceptable to his intelligence by anthropology.

Lawrence had managed to combine what had never been combined and, if not to reconcile, at least to suppress the elements that worst confounded his confusion. But however odd their confusion may at first appear, animism and theosophy are not ill assorted. One is primitive, the other primitivistic; a belief in either depends more or less upon the findings of the anthropologists; both offer a suitable release for the soul and allow the correction of materialists. Their quarrel concerns the Oversoul, Anima Mundi, and cyclical reincarnation. This conflict found Lawrence on the side of the animists, and what is not theosophical in his philosophy may be traced to this preference. His rejection of Buddhistic oneness and of Anima Mundi and his general indifference to metempsychosis show at once his choice of animistic polytheism and his confirmed dislike of abstractions or the ideals of other men.

Lawrence's most animistic novel, *The Plumed Serpent,* is also his most theosophical. Its theme is that of Mme Blavatsky's *Secret Doctrine:* the recovery of lost Atlantis by means of myths and symbols. More practical than Mme Blavatsky, however, and not content merely to talk about a primitive Utopia, Don Ramon erects a past Utopia in the present, generally according to Mme Blavatsky's plan, but with modern improvements. The end and means are hers, the improvements Frazer's.

Although it is animistic, Don Ramon's Utopia is Atlantis recaptured. As his plans mature, Kate feels "swept away in some silent tide, to the old, antediluvian silence . . ." As his plans triumph, she feels akin to men of "that old pre-Flood world" before the melting of the glaciers and the immersion of the adept: "When great plains stretched away to the oceans, like Atlantis and the lost continents of Polynesia . . . and the soft, dark-eyed people of that world could walk around the globe. Then there was a mysterious, hot-blooded, soft-footed humanity with a strange civilization of its own." [38] Kate knows that what is aboriginal in Mexico belongs to this world before the Flood. Being Irish, she is in a position to understand the antediluvian; for in the Celtic soul, as in the Mexican, Lawrence observes, lingers the memory of Atlantis. She sees that Don Ramon is trying to effect a fusion between scientific Europe and the life now lying beneath the sea. Such thoughts make it clear that Kate has read the Foreword to Lawrence's *Fantasia,* just as Don Ramon's desire for a fusion between science and Atlantis helps to explain the confusion of anthropology and theosophy in his Utopia.

" 'I would like,' " says the Don, echoing Mme Blavatsky, " 'to be one of the Initiates of the Earth.' " [39] His understanding of the truth shows that he is what he would like to be. He knows that there is one central truth, that all religions are ways to it, and that all prophets such as Buddha, Mohammed, Christ, and Quetzalcoatl pointed consciously or unconsciously to the primitive wisdom. Aware that the way to this mystery

[38] *Plumed Serpent,* pp. 443–44; cf. p. 308.   [39] *Ibid.,* p. 265.

is through ancient myths and symbols, he proposes the revival of local cults and divinities, of Thor, Hermes Trismegistus, Ashtaroth, Mithras, Brahma, and of their symbolic accompaniments of mistletoe, the tree Igdrasil, the bull, and the dragon. " 'The mystery is one mystery,' " he says, " 'but men must see it differently.' " [40] As Yeats the Irishman chose Irish myths and symbols as the way to the central truth, so Don Ramon the Mexican chooses the myth and symbols of Quetzalcoatl as the path to Atlantis. To him, Quetzalcoatl is a symbol of the primitive truth; and, as Yeats found in symbols a magical power, so Don Ramon finds the names of the Mexican gods " 'so full of magic, of the unexplored magic. Huitzilopochtli!—how wonderful!' " he exclaims. " 'And Tlaloc! Ah! I love them! I say them over and over, like they say *Mani padma Om!* in Thibet.' " [41] The magical name of Quetzalcoatl, with its Thibetan significance, does not mean a return to Aztec horrors. Quetzalcoatl serves to recall something before the day of the Aztecs. These people, who had degenerated from Atlantean wisdom, forgot the meaning of the symbols they had preserved. [42]

The incidental symbolism employed by Don Ramon in his cult of Quetzalcoatl is not without esoteric interest. Much of it came from Zelia Nuttall, but she was an archaeologist who, like an Aztec, failed to understand. When Lawrence substituted the morning star for her Polaris, he was moved apparently not alone by the convenience of this planet as a symbol of duality but by

[40] *Ibid.*, pp. 265–66; cf. p. 283.   [41] *Ibid.*, p. 66; cf. pp. 62–63.
[42] *Ibid.*, pp. 66, 132.

Mme Blavatsky's disclosures of the meaning of Venus and her ankh. Quetzalcoatl's favorite symbol, a serpent with its tail in its mouth, is described by Kate as "a curious deviation from the Mexican emblem . . ." [43] This deviation from the Mexican emblem to the favorite symbol of the theosophist is, however, not as curious as Kate absent-mindedly remarked. She should also have seen that the seven triangles which complete Quetzalcoatl's symbol are equally theosophical; for in the Foreword to *Fantasia*, which she seems to have read, Lawrence spoke of mathematic figures and their esoteric meaning; and seven is the numerical key to Blavatsky's system.[44]

"The Great Breath" of Lawrence's Quetzalcoatl [45] was exhaled by Mme Blavatsky. The secret sun behind the sun, which is invoked throughout *The Plumed Serpent*,[46] is Mme Blavatsky's central sun, the soul of all things, of which the apparent sun is only the symbol.[47] Although Lawrence seems elsewhere to have taken little interest in metempsychosis, *The Plumed Serpent* contains several references to the cyclical development of races and to reincarnation under the law of Karma.[48] Most theosophical of all, however, is Hymn Number Four of Don Ramon's hymnal. This rhapsody concerns not only symbolical dragons but the varieties of earthbound spirits and what Mme Blavatsky called elementals: salamanders, for example, and water sprites.

[43] *Ibid.*, p. 127; cf. p. 186.
[44] At Don Ramon's ceremonies seven men symbolically brood.
[45] *Plumed Serpent*, p. 117.   [46] For example, *ibid.*, p. 388.
[47] Lawrence's repudiation of the scientific theory of the sun in *Fantasia* is also an echo of the Master. Cf. "The Crown," *Porcupine*, pp. 99–100.
[48] *Plumed Serpent*, pp. 83, 157, 406, 409.

Indeed, Don Cipriano himself is something of a salamander.[49]

In one of his essays on the novel, written at about the same time as *The Plumed Serpent,* Lawrence said:

> You may be a theosophist, and then you will cry: *Avaunt! Thou dark-red aura! Away!!!—Oh come! Thou pale-blue or thou primrose aura, come!*
> This you may cry if you are a theosophist. And if you put a theosophist in a novel, he or she may cry *avaunt!* to the heart's content.
> But a theosophist cannot be a novelist, as a trumpet cannot be a regimental band. A theosophist, or a Christian, or a Holy Roller, may be *contained* in a novelist.[50]

Besides the unfairness with which Lawrence habitually treated those to whom he was indebted there is much in this passage to interest the critic. After reading *The Plumed Serpent,* the hostile critic might remark that Lawrence was right in saying that a theosophist cannot be a novelist. The tender critic might insist that the theosophist who wrote *The Plumed Serpent* was contained in a novelist.

There are other occult matters in this novel, but before considering them, we must return to Lawrence's acquaintance with India. Although he disliked Buddhism, he approved of Hinduism, which is also included in theosophy. The religion of the *Rigveda,* with its polytheistic nature-worship, won his heart by its resemblance to animism. To be sure, he sometimes expressed enmity to Hinduism as to everything else, but on the whole he found it congenial, as he often told

---

[49] *Ibid.,* pp. 276–77, 342. Cf. earth-bound spirits in *Last Poems,* pp. 63–65, 304–5.
[50] *Porcupine,* pp. 120–21.

Earl Brewster, from whom he learned much about India. "I have always worshipped Shiva," he said. "For me, it is the Hindu, Brahman thing—that queer fluidity, those lively, kicking legs, that attract me: the pre-Buddha." [51] Through Mr. Brewster he met Dhan Gopal Mukerji and other Hindus; and from his Buddhistic friend he borrowed such books as Coomaraswamy's *Dance of Siva* and J. C. Chatterji's *Kashmir Shaivaism.*[52] In his letters to Mr. Brewster, Lawrence tells of the pleasure he found in the Hindu scriptures; and it is clear from a casual allusion in one of these letters that he had read at least parts of the *Vedas* and the *Upanishads.*[53] His creator's interest in Hinduism explains why that spiritual man the gamekeeper in *Lady Chatterley's Lover* kept three books concerning India on his meager bookshelf.[54]

Of the departments of Hinduism, Lawrence, like Thoreau, was particularly fascinated with yoga. What the spiritual exercises of St. Ignatius Loyola are to Christianity, yoga is to Hinduism. Yoga may be described as a system of physical and mental discipline with illumination or mystical experience as its end. By ascetic postures, deep breathing, concentration, and the monotonous repetition of aphorisms, in the way made familiar by Coué, the yogi refines his spirit. By means of his exercises or concentration the adept awakens Kundalini, the serpent power lying coiled and dormant at the base

[51] Brewster, *Reminiscences,* pp. 108, 112; cf. pp. 49, 99, 121, 213, and also *Letters,* pp. 350, 543, 652.

[52] Brewster, *Reminiscences,* p. 175. In 1915 he met his first Hindu: *Letters,* p. 284.

[53] Brewster, *Reminiscences,* pp. 86, 175. See Carter, *Body Mystical,* p. 17, on Lawrence's reading the Vedanta; in *Letters,* p. 350, Lawrence read Manucci's history of India in 1916.

[54] *Lady Chatterley,* p. 255.

of the spine, and sends it upward along the spine through seven centers or chakras to the top of the head and thence to God. The successful yogi gains peace, freedom from the cycle of reincarnation, and the ability to take enemas without mechanical assistance.[55]

In the Foreword to *Fantasia,* during his confession of debt to Frazer, Frobenius, and intuition, Lawrence also admitted a debt to yoga.[56] He did not try to hide his acquaintance with this Hindu discipline from his friends. At their first meeting he discussed the centers or chakras with Mr. Brewster, and he gave Mrs. Luhan useful advice on the awakening of her centers and the unfolding of Kundalini.[57] But any theosophist could have helped Mrs. Luhan in these matters; for yoga is also embraced by theosophy. Mme Blavatsky has a great deal to say about yoga in *The Secret Doctrine,* Mrs. Besant devoted a book to the subject, and the *Upanishads* are informative about the chakras. Lawrence may have owed some of his wisdom to any or to all of these; but he told Mr. Brewster, in answer to a question, that he first became acquainted with yoga through reading *The Apocalypse Unveiled* by an author whose name he could not recall.[58] This work, whose title he confused with *Isis Unveiled,* is *The Apocalypse Unsealed,* 1910,

---

[55] See Arthur Avalon, *The Serpent Power* (London, Luzac, 1919).

[56] *Fantasia,* p. 8.

[57] Brewster, *Reminiscences,* p. 18; Luhan, *Lorenzo in Taos,* pp. 61, 63. By 1929 Mr. Brewster seems to have become more familiar with yoga than he was when Lawrence first spoke to him about it; for in 1929 Lawrence sneered at Mr. Brewster's yoga exercises "which make him hold his breath till his brain goes silly." "Letters of Lawrence to Max Mohr," *T'ien Hsia Monthly,* I (September, 1935), 175.

[58] Brewster, *Reminiscences,* pp. 141–42. I am indebted to Dr. Elliott Dobbie for aid in determining the authorship of *The Apocalypse Unsealed.*

by James M. Pryse. Lawrence's confusion of titles was a happy one; for Pryse is a theosophist who was so close to Mme Blavatsky that, with Mrs. Besant, he was permitted to become one of the dozen inmates of Madame's London household. Hearing about Dublin, he went there, after Mme Blavatsky's death, to reside with Yeats, Johnston, and A.E. in their household. It was Pryse, said A.E., who first instructed him in ceremonial magic and in the mystery of initiation.[59] Still unsatisfied, Pryse moved to Los Angeles. But he had left his mark on English literature. As his occult wisdom had helped to edify A.E., so his book on yoga inspired Lawrence. Judging by his reference to other writers,[60] Lawrence read more books than one on the subject, but Pryse's had a profound and lasting effect on him, one that may be traced in most of the books he wrote after 1920.

Though Pryse does not mention yoga, his book deals with the control of the electrical life-force, which is symbolized by a serpent and is known as Kundalini in the *Upanishads*, and with the seven principal centers or chakras along the spine, located in the ganglia of the sympathetic nervous system. From the chakra of the loins, through those of the navel and the heart, into that of the head, the positive and negative, the solar and lunar, forces of Kundalini rise until they become the

[59] Besant, *Autobiography*, p. 361; letter from A.E., published in *The Canadian Theosophist*, XVI (August, 1935), 166: I owe *The Canadian Theosophist* citation to one of my former students, Miss Elizabeth Jorzick, an authority on A.E.

[60] Brewster, *Reminiscences*, pp. 141–42. Lawrence says that Pryse is cited by other writers on yoga. One such reference occurs in Avalon's *Serpent Power*, which Mrs. Lawrence has told me that Lawrence did not read. But, she added, "he would have loved it."

Great Breath, symbolized by the moon. At his initiation to the mysteries, the candidate for spiritual rebirth learns to control Kundalini and send it through the chakras to the pineal center. His Third Eye opened, he immediately becomes alive to spiritual reality. Of this important book Lawrence said: "It's not important. But it gave me the first clue." [61]

He developed this clue in his usual eclectic way in *Psychoanalysis and the Unconscious.* The debt owed by this book to Herakleitos has been mentioned, but in my earlier chapters the question of Lawrence's sources was not fully answered. Pryse's book completes the answer. That knowledge of the unconscious and its centers which Lawrence ascribed to intuition came from Pryse. "Having begun to explore the unconscious," said Lawrence in *Psychoanalysis,* "we find we must go from centre to centre, chakra to chakra, to use an old esoteric word." [62] Of Pryse's seven chakras, he adopted four. He followed Pryse's identification of these centers with the ganglia of the sympathetic nervous system and his idea of the positive and negative electrical currents running through and awakening them. But Lawrence changed the flow of Pryse's life-force or Kundalini from upward to outward and put it to the uses of polarity. Pryse does not mention polarity, a word which, as I have suggested, Lawrence may have found in Emerson. But a likelier source is Pryse's master, Mme Blavatsky, who, in *The Secret Doctrine,* discusses the positive and negative polarity of Fohat the electrical life-force. Taking what he wanted from Pryse, Blavatsky, and the Greeks, Law-

[61] Brewster, *Reminiscences,* pp. 141–42.   [62] Page 90.

rence adapted it to his ideal of animistic contact with
the universe. His theory of the unconscious, like all else
in his system, is a mixture of strange elements, but it is
so much indebted to Pryse that it might be called modified yoga. At the end of his book, Lawrence admitted,
in a way which once more shows this debt, that his treatment of the chakras was incomplete:

Still remain to be revealed the other great centres of the
unconscious. We know four: two pairs. In all there are
seven planes. That is, there are six dual centres of spon-
taneous polarity, and then the final one. That is, the great
upper and lower consciousness is only just broached—
the further heights and depths are not even hinted at.
Nay, in public it would hardly be allowed us to hint at
them.[63]

In *Fantasia*, however, Lawrence dared to tell. He
added two upper and two lower centers, and he hinted
at the existence of another. This final one, the seat of
the pineal eye, is in the head. Although he accepted the
Third Eye elsewhere, here Lawrence felt compelled to
omit everything above the neck, sacrificing Vedantic
truth in order to remain true to the theory of mindlessness which this book was designed to promote.[64] This
further distortion is atoned for, however, by Pryse's
theory of the lunar and solar connections of the ganglia,
which Lawrence accepted and was able to elaborate by
the aid of Mme Blavatsky's ideas on the spiritual sun and
moon. "Let us pronounce the mystic Om, from the pit
of the stomach, and proceed . . ." Lawrence playfully

[63] *Psychoanalysis*, pp. 127–28.
[64] At their first meeting, Lawrence advised Mr. Brewster not to be
governed by this center between the eyebrows but rather by the center
of the solar plexus: Brewster, *Reminiscences*, p. 18.

remarked, and, with unusual candor, he added, "All I say is Om!" [65]

Several of his friends recognized *Psychoanalysis and the Unconscious* for what it is. Upon receiving his copy, Mr. Brewster at once knew it to be an interpretation, "by a genius," of the ancient Hindu idea of the chakras.[66] Although he did not know the exact source of Lawrence's ideas, Mr. Frederick Carter surmised that Lawrence had found his seven centers in some American book on the Vedanta.[67] In America, Mrs. Luhan read *Psychoanalysis,* found her centers to be unawakened, and invited the British yogi to pay her a visit.[68]

As Mrs. Luhan had foreseen, America gave Lawrence an opportunity to spread the news about yoga. In *Aaron's Rod* he had mentioned the power at the base of the spine; and Birkin of *Women in Love* had known, as a carven Egyptian statue knows, what it is to have this magical, mystical force along his backbone.[69] But, as Lawrence said in one of his essays, the solar plexus had a better chance in Mexico.[70] In *The Plumed Serpent,* Lawrence took this chance and made the most of it.

The spiritual exercises which Don Ramon performs in the darkness of his room were inspired by those of the yogi. Filling his mind with the darkness of his room, this initiate mindlessly concentrates. He feels the fe-

---

[65] *Fantasia,* p. 16. Even his apparent ignorance of yoga failed to prevent J. Middleton Murry from considering *Fantasia* the wisest, profoundest, and best of Lawrence's works: *Son of Woman,* pp. 152–79; cf. pp. 1, 123, 177.

[66] Brewster, *Reminiscences,* p. 27.   [67] *Body Mystical,* p. 25.

[68] *Lorenzo in Taos,* pp. 11–12.

[69] *Aaron's Rod,* p. 94; *Women in Love,* pp. 81, 363–65; cf. *Porcupine,* pp. 133, 152; *Mornings in Mexico,* p. 148; *Letters,* p. 558.

[70] *Phoenix,* p. 104.

cundity of an inner tide washing over his heart and belly, which are thereby restored, and his tension sends the arrows of his soul to dissolve in the greater dark mind. " 'My belly,' " says the Don, " 'is a flood of power, that races in down the sluice of bone at my back.' " [71] These exercises give him the power and wisdom to initiate his friend Don Cipriano into the mystery. At this ceremony, which is modeled roughly upon the initiations described by Pryse and Mme Blavatsky, one Don binds the other until he is helpless, then placing his hands on the other's breast, shoulders, heart, navel, back, and loins induces a trance in which Cipriano converses with the source of all things.[72] The new initiate, like the old, can now control the "sleeping or waking serpent in the bellies of men," and he enjoys that strange old power in his spine.[73] He has been reborn.

According to Pryse, initiation concerns the control of Kundalini, the serpent coiled at the base of the spine; and by good fortune, the Aztec Quetzalcoatl was a plumed serpent. Lawrence knew, of course, what anthropologists like Frazer, Frobenius, and Nuttall had said about the serpent symbol. Lawrence's Quetzalcoatl, however, is not the god misunderstood by anthropologists and Aztecs, whatever features he inherited from him, nor is he merely a convenient symbol of the lifeforce, but, reborn with his tail in his mouth, he has become Pryse's Kundalini. Lawrence's improved deity says: " 'When the snake of your body lifts its head, beware! It is I, Quetzalcoatl, rearing up in you, rearing up and

[71] *Plumed Serpent*, p. 193.   [72] *Ibid.*, pp. 181–82, 207, 392–95.
[73] *Ibid.*, pp. 401, 428.

reaching beyond the bright day, to the sun of darkness beyond, where is your home at last. . . . And I am not with you till my serpent has coiled his circle of rest in your belly.' " [74] The orthodox Aztec might be surprised to find that Quetzalcoatl was really Kundalini, but the theosophist, knowing that Hindus and Aztecs are of one primitive faith, could not but be pleased with Lawrence's discovery.

It should be apparent by now that Lawrence's *Apocalypse* is a theosophical tract. His quest of primitive truth through the symbols of the Book of Revelation, their meaning hidden beneath Christian corruptions from all but the esoteric eye, is one which Mme Blavatsky had pursued before him in *The Secret Doctrine*. Elaborating her discoveries, Pryse had said in his *Apocalypse Unsealed* that beneath the language of Revelation, as beneath that of the *Upanishads,* lies a common esoteric doctrine, involving Kundalini and the seven chakras and known to Greek as to Hindu initiates. The Apocalypse, he continued, tells of John's initiation into this wisdom. The seven seals of Revelation are the chakras, the dragon is Kundalini, and the horses, stars, and numbers fall as readily into the occult pattern. Though it owes much to John Burnet's *Early Greek Philosophy*, Lawrence's *Apocalypse* is essentially a close adaptation of Pryse and Blavatsky. In their books he found what he had to say about the numbers three, four, and seven, about the seven seals, about the four beasts, man, lion, bull, and eagle, which had inspired some of his verses, and about initiation, which, follow-

[74] *Ibid.,* pp. 132, 368; cf. pp. 189, 244, 391, 401.

ing Pryse, he made the central theme of the Apocalypse.[75] Fascinated by initiation, Lawrence described the emergence of John's Kundalini, the awakening of his six centers, and, with the breaking of the seventh seal, his rebirth, the opening of his Third Eye, and his communion with the Infinite. It is not odd, considering Lawrence's dependence upon Pryse, that the initiation of Don Cipriano should have been similar to John's; nor is it surprising that the dragon of Revelation should be the same as Quetzalcoatl. This dragon, whose liberation was the principal problem of the good old days, Lawrence also found to be identical with that of the Chinese and with that which "according to the Hindus, coils quiescent at the base of the spine of a man, and unfolds sometimes lashing along the spinal way: and the yogi is only trying to set this dragon in controlled motion." [76]

Apocalypse, which is thus enriched, is enriched beyond Pryse by astrology. In *Psychoanalysis* Lawrence had referred to the astrological correspondence between the microcosm and the macrocosm, and in *Fantasia* he had denied that astrology is nonsense.[77] Even an unintuitive theosophist, however, would know that much; for

[75] *Apocalypse,* pp. 42, 54, 62, 63, 92, 96, 97, 102, 104, 108–10, 158, 164, 166, 171. That Lawrence read Pryse before 1919 is shown by Lawrence's remarks on the centers of the unconscious in the first version of his essay on Fenimore Cooper in *The English Review,* XXVIII (February, 1919), 89–90. Here Lawrence follows Pryse in saying that a knowledge of the centers was possessed by an esoteric priesthood, taught in initiations to the Eleusinian mysteries, and concealed in the symbols of John's Apocalypse. These essays of 1918–19 on American literature were the first drafts of Lawrence's *Fantasia* and *Apocalypse.* See *The English Review,* XXVIII (June, 1919), 488: ". . . and there is the great living plexus of the loins, there where deep calls to deep."

[76] *Apocalypse,* p. 146; cf. pp. 142, 144, 145, 149.

[77] *Psychoanalysis,* p. 51; *Fantasia,* p. 146. Cf. Knud Merrild, *A Poet and Two Painters,* p. 312.

theosophy, of course, includes astrology. But Lawrence did not have to depend upon Mme Blavatsky for his feelings about the stars. In 1923 Frederick Carter, the nontheosophical astrologer, sent Lawrence the manuscript of his *Dragon of the Alchemists,* which by virtue of its obscurity, Lawrence said, gave him spiritual comfort and enlarged his imagination. The living universe of Chaldea, which he found here, was far more exciting than the dead universe of astronomy.[78] On his visit to England early in 1924, Lawrence stayed with Carter in Shropshire for several days. This visit is celebrated in *St. Mawr,* where Carter appears as Cartwright, a master of the occult who is able to see Pan with his Third Eye.[79] During this visit Lawrence and Carter discussed alchemy, dragons, symbols, stars, and the soul.[80] Inspired by such considerations, Lawrence composed an essay "On Being Religious," which concerns the precession of the equinoxes. The two initiates planned to write jointly on the astrological symbols of the Book of Revelation, Lawrence to compose the preface, Carter the part that remained. Lawrence wrote a short preface, which was published posthumously in *The London Mercury* and in *Phoenix,* but he discarded this for a more ambitious one, which turned into a book. In 1929, during Lawrence's last illness, Carter visited his collaborator in the South of France,[81] to discuss their collaboration. The astrologer explained the apocalyptic theories of Dupuis and introduced Lawrence to the Book of Enoch. But as Lawrence had pondered Revelation, his growing

[78] *Phoenix,* pp. 292 ff.   [79] *Tales,* pp. 598, 599, 600, 601.
[80] Carter, *Body Mystical,* pp. 5, 34.
[81] *Ibid.,* pp. 43, 53, 60, 61, 62; *Letters,* p. 840.

preface to Carter's *Dragon of Revelation* departed more
and more from astrological orthodoxy. Disappointed
that Lawrence was unwilling or unable to master the
subject as a serious student should, Carter complained
that Vedantic elements and the quest of Atlantis had
impaired Lawrence's vision of the stars.[82] Death interrupted their unfortunate divergence. Carter published
his book without Lawrence's preface, and Lawrence's
literary executors published the once prefatory *Apocalypse* without mentioning Carter. There was little need,
however, to mention him; for what had started as a
preface to his work had ended by being a sequel to
Pryse's. Although Carter's ideas on the zodiac and the
macrocosm occasionally appear in *Apocalypse*,[83] Lawrence used them for theosophical purposes; and Carter's
stellar dragon had served merely to increase the splendor
of Kundalini by which it was obscured. Lawrence's experience with illiberal astrology had left him an eclectic
theosophist.[84]

As even the most casual theosophist knows, the cow
was a religious object to Egyptians, Babylonians, and
early Hindus. In *The Secret Doctrine*, Mme Blavatsky
speaks of the cow as a symbol so occult that, although it
could not be fully understood until the fourth initiation, it was universally adored. To the Hindu, she said,

[82] Carter, *Body Mystical*, pp. 19–20, 53, 54, 61.

[83] *Apocalypse*, pp. 43, 45, 57, 90. Cf. astrological allusions in *Last
Poems*, pp. 18, 130.

[84] The story of the involved relationship of Lawrence and Carter,
with natural emphasis upon Carter's side, may be found in: Carter,
D. H. Lawrence and the Body Mystical; "Note by the Publisher," in
Carter, *The Dragon of Revelation.* See also Edward D. McDonald,
Introduction to *Phoenix*, pp. xviii–xix; "Letters of Lawrence to Max
Mohr," *T'ien Hsia Monthly,* I (September, 1935), 175.

the female principle of nature was represented as Vâch, "the melodious cow." The cow's horns of Isis identify her with Vâch, continued Mme Blavatsky. Hence Isis is "mystic, though physical, Nature, with all her magic ways and properties." What is more: "The ceremony of passing through the Holy of Holies (now symbolized by the cow) . . . meant spiritual conception and . . . the re-birth of the individual . . ." [85] It is clear that to Mme Blavatsky, who had unveiled her, Isis or Nature itself was symbolized by the cow; and the cow, like the moon, the morning star, the phoenix, and the serpent, meant occult rebirth, initiation, or the union of spirit and matter. It would be unreasonable to suppose that Mme Blavatsky's bovine disclosures were rejected by Lawrence, who had received her serpent and, probably, her phoenix and her morning star and who was fascinated by rebirth and initiation as she and her disciples described them. Indeed, her disclosures were corroborated by his experience; for through the centers of his breast and abdomen, like an Egyptian or a child, he could perceive "the fearful and wonderful elements of the cow-form, which the dynamic soul perfectly perceives." [86] Susan, who wonderfully reclined before his dynamic soul "like a black Hindu statue," [87] had an esoteric as well as a primitive significance. When Mme Blavatsky unveiled Isis,[88] she unveiled for Lawrence the pastured sym-

[85] *Secret Doctrine*, I, 434; II, 470. For Mme Blavatsky on cows, see *ibid.*, I, 67, 137, 390; II, 31; and *Isis Unveiled* (New York, J. W. Bouton, 1891), I, 147, 262–63.

[86] *Fantasia*, p. 81; cf. p. 58.   [87] *Porcupine*, p. 164; cf. p. 187.

[88] Lawrence's Jesus in "The Man Who Died" is converted to the truth by a priestess of Isis (*Tales*, pp. 1118, 1120), who owes as much to Blavatsky as to Frazer. Afterwards, Jesus feels reborn and announces

bol of Isis, through which Isis and what lay beyond her could be approached. Only the most occidental bird on that sole Arabian tree could complain that the turtle of our Phoenix was a cow.

---

that "the gold and flowing serpent is coiling up again, to sleep at the root of my tree" (p. 1138). Isis had awakened Kundalini.

CHAPTER SIX

LAWRENCE AMONG THE FASCISTS

LAWRENCE saw that the civilization of the middle classes was disorderly and ill adapted to cow-worship. As a politician he longed to impose order upon confusion. As an evangelist he wanted to share his faith with others, indeed to impose it upon them. To these ends he proposed a new society in which theosophy, animism, and dancing to the drum would be congenial and Susan would receive her due. This may sound harmless enough, but the social, political, and economic remedy which he prescribed for the world has caused Nazis to hail him as one of their number and has led several Marxist or independent critics such as John Strachey, Newton Arvin, and Ernest Seillière to describe Lawrence as a fascist or at least a proto-fascist.[1] But many Marxists find him agreeable. Stephen Spender and C. Day Lewis appear to admire him as much for helping to free their generation from a stale past as the Germans adore him for his part in reviving a stale past.[2] Even to certain Trotskyites of my acquaintance Lawrence seems all but a fellow traveler. Such variety of description, which cannot be ascribed entirely to sec-

[1] Anselm Schlösser, *Die englische Literatur in Deutschland von 1895 bis 1934* (Jena, Biedermann, 1937); John Strachey, *Literature and Dialectical Materialism*, pp. 16–19; Newton Arvin, "D. H. Lawrence and Fascism," *The New Republic*, Vol. LXXXIX (December 16, 1936).

[2] Stephen Spender, "Notes on D. H. Lawrence," *The Destructive Element;* C. Day Lewis, "A Hope for Poetry," *Collected Poems.*

tarian heat or to loose usage, is hardly surprising; for Lawrence was often so inconsistent about politics that it is not easy to discover what his position was. His attitude of disapproval toward present society, his solemnity of tone, and his enthusiasm, all of which seem to be fatal to critical detachment, have enabled readers of all sorts to impute their own political sentiments or antipathies to him. Although some of his critics have come near the mark, none has hit it exactly.

Lawrence's ideas of society took shape during the war, when capitalism and science seemed to have embraced each other in a disorderly dance of death. The war convinced Lawrence, as it convinced many other men, that the present system was doomed. He saw money and ownership as agents and symbols of destruction, not only of capitalism itself but of man. His ignorance of economics did not keep him from seeing that some social and economic change was needed if man was to survive. In one of his last essays he expressed this conviction with something less than his earlier vehemence:

There is a great change coming, bound to come. The whole money arrangement will undergo a change: what, I don't know. The whole industrial system will undergo a change. Work will be different. Class will be different. . . . I know a change is coming—and I know we must have a more generous, more human system based on the life values and not on the money values.[3]

Although he added that as a novelist "change inside the individual" was his real concern, it is plain that like H. G. Wells and many other writers of our day he had been compelled by the economic and social disorders

[3] *Assorted Articles,* pp. 97–98.

of the world to emerge from the novelist's province and direct the blast.

Lawrence's own economic position goes far toward explaining the bitterness of his feeling against the present system. His parents were very poor. Young Lawrence faced the alternative of becoming a miner or a clerk. He chose the latter, and for his services to a manufacturer of surgical instruments he received thirteen shillings a week. Freed at last from the forceps by the award of a government scholarship, Lawrence became, upon his graduation from a teachers' college, an ill-paid schoolteacher at Croydon. When he abandoned teaching and eloped with Frieda in 1912, he had about fifty pounds in his pocket, the proceeds from *The Trespasser*. He proposed to live by his writing. For years, however, the money he received for his books and articles or from his friends was hardly sufficient to supply his barest needs. Some of his books were banned or denied publication. His American publisher failed. But after the war the gradual success of his writings brought him to a state of such comparative affluence that he had money not only to travel around the world but to invest and lose in the stock market of 1929. Affluence did nothing, however, to diminish that hatred of money and private ownership which poverty and the war had once inspired and which his antimaterialistic sentiments had helped to preserve. In his novels and letters Lawrence continued to prophesy doom to the moneychangers and to pray for a violent revolution to drive them from the temple.

Financial independence also failed to deaden his

memory of the capitalistic treadmill of miners, clerks, and teachers from which he had escaped. In his *Last Poems* he thinks with horror and despair of the "industrial millions," "the men of the masses," living on inadequate wages in squalid cottages or, what is worse, in cities, enslaved by machines and drugged by the cinema.[4] As he sat among the flowers, the social outlaw, as he called himself, made himself miserable by thinking of unluckier men in cities. He thought of dismal crowds in London. He shuddered at the thought of West 50th Street, of West 100th Street, of Westchester businessmen in trains. "I care nothing for New York," he exclaimed, "and don't get much out of New Jersey."[5]

He reserved those simple Anglo-Saxon words of which he was fond for comment upon the rich, whom he held responsible for cities, factories, and the sufferings of the poor.[6] As a gesture of contempt toward the society of the capitalists and all its ways, he sometimes blew his nose in the letters he received—an aristocratic friend, who was solicitous of his convenience, wrote letters to him on the softest tissues. And in recognition of his gestures many Marxists have applauded his "destructive" attitude.

Such applause might seem better justified by Lawrence's habit of placing the villains of his novels in the upper classes, the heroes in the lower. Lifeless, corrupt, and intellectual characters like the well-born Hermione and Lord Chatterley, whose paralysis also has a social significance, are foils for vital plebeians like Birkin and

---

[4] *Last Poems*, pp. 167, 168, 172.   [5] *Letters*, pp. 324, 574, 576.
[6] Frieda Lawrence, *"Not I, but the Wind . . . ,"* p. 159.

Mellors, the gamekeeper, who deliberately uses the dialect of the lower classes to disconcert his elegant mistress. Even before Lawrence had met any representatives of the gentry, he depicted plutocratic mine-owners in *The White Peacock* as disagreeable intellectuals, addicted to quoting Latin. Lawrence liked gamekeepers and peasants not only because they quoted no Latin and were close to nature but because they were of the lower orders, perfectly qualified for the salvation of the heroine of rank and title from the disadvantages of her class. Miners were capable of similar services. Aaron, the discontented coal miner of *Aaron's Rod*, abandons his class, as Lawrence had done before him, to consort with aristocrats, but he notices that the higher the rank and the greater the wealth of those he meets the more mechanical and moribund they are. The vicar in "The Daughters of the Vicar" prides himself upon "belonging indisputably to the upper or ordering classes" and depends upon his position in society to give him a position among men. This wicked man learns from his daughter, who runs away with a miner, that life is more important than class. Lewis, the groom in *St. Mawr*, is a mere servant, but, as Lawrence says of this plebeian saviour of heiresses, real power and distinction go unrecognized in our artificial society. Even Count Psanek, the dark little saviour of Lady Daphne in "The Ladybird," is not the aristocrat he seems; for he comes of a race of prehistoric slaves. Until disarmed by this little man, or by his title perhaps, Lady Daphne has been prevented by the gulf between the classes from succumbing to the gamekeepers by whom she is enchanted. Her heart has always told her, however, that the lower or "unconscious classes," unlike the upper, think with their blood.[7]

Social allegories of this sort reflect the class consciousness which was to be expected of a miner's son who had instructed, saved, and married the daughter of a baron. Lawrence's heroes are often as class-conscious as Lawrence was. The hero of "Glad Ghosts," for example, never forgets the social chasm between himself and his aristocratic friends. But however aware of his origin and however given to allegories of caste, Lawrence did not count himself among the workers from whom he had sprung, though in moments of sentiment he could call them "flesh of my flesh." Like Somers, the hero of *Kangaroo,* he had risen, by the aid of his talents, to a position of social ambiguity in which he was at home with members of no class. Naturally the middle classes, whose control of money and machines he detested, failed to suit him. Nor was he more at ease among the gentry, with whom he preferred to live, than among the workers, whom he could neither forget nor accept. In his "Autobiographical Sketch" he tells of his predicament: "Class makes a gulf, across which the best human flow is lost. . . . As a man from the working class, I feel that the middle class cut off some of my vital vibration when I am with them. . . . Then why don't I live with my working people? Because . . . . the working class is narrow in outlook. . . . One can belong absolutely to no class." [8] He was not one, he added, to follow Barrie and

[7] *The White Peacock,* p. 347; *Aaron's Rod,* pp. 181, 192, 211, 231; *Tales,* pp. 47, 375, 402, 408, 588, 596.
[8] *Assorted Articles,* pp. 152, 153.

Wells from the lower to the middle class. He would remain classless, uprooted, and alone.

Democracy, the government favored by the middle and lower classes, was no more acceptable to him than the classes themselves. His social and economic troubles and the war had convinced him of the failure of democracy. Liberty and equality, he announced, are dead ideals, resulting in disorder and, although this may seem odd, destructive of individualism. His soul could not expand under the weight of the democratic mob.[9]

Socialism seemed to him to have all the disadvantages of democracy. In his youth, Lawrence had been attracted to the Fabians and the Labor Party, and he had delivered an address before the socialists of Croydon, but by 1910 he had found the socialists stupid and flat.[10] Later he began to consider them materialistic and mechanical. In Italy and Mexico, during the 1920's, he regarded the activities of the militant socialists with anxiety. He hated the strikes forced upon the workers by social idealists, who, in their way, were as bad as the capitalists.[11] Under socialists and capitalists alike he saw men of the working class becoming horrible, soulless creatures like ants or bees:

> Oh I have loved the working class
> where I was born,
> and lived to see them spawn into machine-robots.[12]

The discouraged poet had prayed for a revolution, but

9 *Letters,* pp. 235, 243, 318; *Phoenix,* p. 699 ff.; *Fantasia,* p. 75; *Sea and Sardinia,* pp. 114, 130.

10 *Letters,* p. 4. But see *ibid.,* pp. 511–12: in 1921 he felt for a moment like joining the revolutionary socialists. This was a passing fancy.

11 *Sea and Sardinia,* pp. 140, 163, 203; *Letters,* p. 622.

12 *Last Poems,* p. 197.

if revolution meant the rule of the incompetent "robot-masses" and their leaders, he preferred to remain in the hands of the bourgeoisie because they would bother him less. Communist Russia, like the democratic world, seemed to him to be founded on the ownership and control of land and machines. He considered Marx more capitalistic than the capitalists; and in *Apocalypse,* where he condemned the envious masses and found them inimical to individuality, he called Lenin evil.[13] What Lawrence wanted was a new world of men, not of robots, a new world of what he called life, not another world like the present in kind. He wanted salvation from robots, property, and machines:

> O! start a revolution, somebody!
> Not to instal the working classes,
> But to abolish the working classes for ever
> And have a world of men.[14]

The polity with which Lawrence hoped to save society and make it suitable for his religious exercises was as obvious as it has become familiar. Like many of his contemporaries, who were also aware of confusion and as acutely certain of the failure of democracy, Lawrence proposed the remedy of dictatorship, not dictatorship by the masses, however, but by a hero. The masses, he announced in 1915, had shown themselves unfit to govern or to elect their governors; and the big-business men had failed to exhibit the honor, glory, and responsibility which is to be expected of leaders. A dictator would

[13] *Apocalypse,* p. 25. See also *ibid.,* Chapters II, IV, XXIII; *Last Poems,* p. 256; *Porcupine,* pp. 112, 117, 156; *Phoenix,* pp. 196, 285, 288, 395, 709; *Assorted Articles,* p. 213.
[14] *Letters,* p. 772.

bring order to the world and restore glory to the people, who, polarized to him, would live by blood alone, after the fashion of primitive man. Unconsciously the people recognized their need. It was Lawrence's duty to make them conscious of it. "Leaders—," he proclaimed, "this is what mankind is craving for." [15]

This fashionable taste for heroes and supermen seems to have been nourished upon the same course of reading and music which had inspired a similar inclination in Bernard Shaw. While still very young, Lawrence was fascinated with those nineteenth-century prophets who had suggested heroic antidotes to democracy. Of Lawrence's early passion for Carlyle and Nietzsche, E. T. has told us in her memoir.[16] And as for Wagner, if we are to credit the evidence of *The Trespasser*, Lawrence's Wagnerian novel, no one, not even Der Fuehrer, expanding in a purified Salzburg, was ever more devoted to the Master. But, unlike Wagner's Siegfried, Lawrence's dictator was more than violent and noisy. He was also vital and, like Wordsworth's Lucy, familiar with sun and shower; for nineteenth-century nature-lovers, vitalists, and theosophists were among his ancestors, and in his capacious chest beat the heart of the noble savage. This sublime individual was Nature's choice. By her he was filled with the true spiritual power and glory of the Living Sun, not with the false material and mental power of Henry Ford or of Lenin. As Nature gave him genuine power so Nature would give him a suitable so-

---

[15] *Fantasia*, p. 78; cf. p. 165, and also *Letters*, pp. 235, 243, 244, 312, 358; *Phoenix*, p. 290; *Porcupine*, p. 151.

[16] For Nietzsche see *Aaron's Rod*, p. 345; *Tales*, p. 796; *Twilight in Italy*, *passim*.

ciety over which to exercise it. Money and ownership would disappear. The old artificial classes of democracy and socialism—the proletariat, the capitalists, and the doubtful people—were to be succeeded by a natural system of rulers and ruled. Some, said Lawrence in his *Porcupine* essays, are born to rule, others to obey. Natural aristocrats, whose power also came from the Living Sun, would carry out the commands of the leader. Lewis, the groom in *St. Mawr,* was one of these natural aristocrats: "Right in the middle of him he accepted something from destiny, that gave him a quality of eternity. . . . In his own odd way he was an aristocrat, inaccessible in his aristocracy. But it was the aristocracy of the invisible powers, the greater influences, nothing to do with human society." [17] After the aristocrats came those upon whom Nature had not bestowed her powers with equal hand, inferiors who, as Lawrence says in *Fantasia,* could be trained for their humble tasks in workshops and schools of manual training. Ideas must be kept from these creatures and action must be substituted for thought. These natural proletarians, drawn from all the present classes, were to find their happiness in obedience to the leader, whom Jews might hiss and infidels abhor.[18]

At first Lawrence had dreamed of equal love for men, women, flowers, and cows. Love for love was to work a universal revolution in society. But as marriage taught him the virtues of domestic tyranny so, during the war, the errors of capitalism and democracy showed him the need of power and glory before love could triumph in

[17] *Tales*, p. 654.

[18] *Porcupine*, pp. 145–58, 224–40; *Fantasia*, pp. 68, 77, 104; *Phoenix*, pp. 587–662.

society as in his home. His postwar novels reveal a change of emphasis from equality to heroic power. Woman's place, he announced, was in the home, her proper concern was with perambulators and groceries, not with votes and politics.[19] His heroes, now at last far lordlier than their ladies, begin to covet power over men as well as women.

Lilly, the hero of *Aaron's Rod*, 1922, believes that the masses and the capitalists must be controlled if society is to be delivered from the "bee-disease" of socialism and democracy. The mode of love and equality, he says, is now exhausted and men desire to obey a leader. Seeing himself in this capacity, he starts his career in a modest way with one follower. One follower, however, is more than falls to the share of Count Psanek of "The Lady-bird," 1923, although this hero speaks persuasively about the sacredness of power, obedience, and faith and enjoys visions of the masses submitting with eagerness and joy to the man of greatest soul. This great-souled Czechoslovakian is more tolerant of obedience than of criticism, but it hardly matters since, in his privacy, he receives neither. In *Kangaroo*, 1923, the leader of men emerges from solitude and confronts his destiny. Somers, who is dissatisfied with the democracy of England, examines and declines the socialism of Australia. Then he is attracted to the system of Kangaroo, a Jewish dema-gogue, who commands a private army with which he hopes to illustrate wisdom, power, and authority to the "ant men," the democrats and communists, before he undertakes their destruction. His followers regard him

19 *Letters*, p. 244.

as a father, his polity as a church. Being bossed by him, says one of his lieutenants, is better than being bossed by international Reds or by international Jewish financiers.[20]

Kangaroo's authority is imperfect, however, compared with that of Don Ramon in *The Plumed Serpent*, 1926. Contemplating the Mexicans with the compassion of one cat watching another cat eat the canary, he finds the people oppressed by socialists, Catholics, and international financiers. Amid popular silence he detects a popular cry for authority, glory, and real religion. He is prepared to gratify the people. The socialists, who display "the hate of the materialistic *have-nots* for the materialistic *haves*," have tried to save the body; he will save the soul, not as the Catholics attempt to save it (for they have no understanding of such things) but in a better way. To take the place of international Catholicism he proposes a national religion for every country, worship of Quetzalcoatl for the Mexicans, of Siegfried, *Das Wurm*, and the Wagnerian pantheon for the Germans. As local pontiff he spreads his national faith in Mexico by broadsides, sermons, ancient symbols, and primitive dances on what would be the village greens if Mexico were a greener country. For the bullfights of the democratic Mexicans he substitutes the adoration of bulls and other symbolic beasts. He has made the world safe for cow-worship. His most potent argument for these reforms is his private militia, composed of natural aristocrats of the Living Sun Behind the Sun, who, at

[20] *Aaron's Rod*, pp. 327, 340, 347; *Tales*, pp. 398–401; *Kangaroo*, pp. 24, 99, 100, 105, 120, 121, 131, 166, 208–9, 337–39.

their leader's appearance, raise their right arms in salute
and ambiguously exclaim "Oye! Oye! Oye!" Through
the aid of one of his aristocrats, who happens to be a
general, Don Ramon gets control of the regular army.
The Catholics, socialists, and international financiers
are expelled or destroyed, and the happy Mexicans defer
to the religious superman.[21] "If I were dictator . . ."
Lawrence had said several years before the triumph of
Don Ramon, "I should have judges with sensitive, living
hearts: not abstract intellects. And because the instinctive heart recognized a man as evil, I would have
that man destroyed. Quickly. Because good warm life is
now in danger." [22]

These fancies pleased Lawrence during the early
1920's; in 1928, however, illness and disillusionment
with Mexico temporarily weakened his faith in leadership. This business of leaders and followers, he wrote to
a friend, is very tiresome; [23] and in *Lady Chatterley's
Lover* of that disappointing year he returned to tenderness and love. But in *Apocalypse,* his last work, he found
comfort again in thoughts of leadership, ecclesiastical
polity, and power.

His yearning for authority and obedience, his hatred
of socialists, Catholics, and international financiers, his
national religions with their pagan rites, his propaganda,
symbols, and storm troopers, his attitude toward women
and laborers, his desire to think with his blood, and the

21 *Plumed Serpent,* pp. 55, 78, 87, 120, 204, 212, 224, 265, 266, 359,
362, 449 ff.
22 *Sea and Sardinia,* p. 27; cf. p. 164 where he prefers nationalism to
proletarian internationalism.
23 *Letters,* p. 711.

other ways in which he anticipated Hitler appear to justify those who have regarded Lawrence as a proto-fascist. So Lawrence seemed to Ernest Seillière, who has pointed out what he considers Lawrence's indebtedness to German pre-Hitlerite writers, like Bachofen, Bleib-treu, and Ludwig Klages.[24] It is true that Lawrence resembles such thinkers-with-the-blood, but M. Seillière has no evidence except Lawrence's marriage to a German and his visits to Germany upon which to base a connection with these philosophers. M. Seillière, who has made the error of confusing similarity with origin, would have a stronger case if he had any evidence to support it. It is likely that the ideas of Lawrence and the Germans are parallel products of identical causes; Lawrence and the Germans had found themselves in the same world and their solutions for its troubles were so obvious and natural under the circumstances that no one need be surprised at their resemblance. Tyranny is an obvious antidote for democratic disorder; and violence, blood, and power are natural antidotes for too much science and intellect.

What M. Seillière noted with rage, Rolf Gardiner, a British fascist, observed with approval. During the 1920's Gardiner became interested in the German youth movement. He spent his holidays moving youths from place to place around Germany and England, pausing at intervals to sing songs, to dance morris dances with the lads, and to remind them that *Kraft durch Freude* was what they were after. The Boy Scouts had failed to

[24] Ernest Seillière, *David-Herbert Lawrence et les récentes idéologies allemandes.* Of course, Lawrence knew the work of Nietzsche, Steiner, and Frobenius, all of whom had some influence upon the Nazis.

satisfy him, and Oswald Mosley, though better than Baden-Powell, had also seemed inadequate. But the works of Lawrence contained what Gardiner was looking for. Here he found an all but Germanic insistence upon leadership, vitality, and mindlessness. He wrote to Lawrence in 1924. Recognizing an affinity, Lawrence replied; and letters continued to pass between them until 1928. Lawrence immediately saw in Gardiner's plans a way to destroy civilization. For years, he said, he had looked for some such movement to belong to, and he wished he were in England instead of Mexico so that he might dance with Gardiner's Nordics, the only people, he added inconsistently, to whom one could look for real guts. Gardiner sent Lawrence a German tract,[25] a book on primitive man, and *The Confession of the Kibbo Kift*, 1927, a work by John Hargrave, successively the leader of the Lonecraft Boys and the Kibbo Kift Kindred, who believed that tyranny and the nationalization of capital would follow upon outdoor discipline, appropriate symbolism, and prophesying before boys. Lawrence read this work with interest, and he admitted that Hargrave had the right idea. But Hargrave was too cold and intellectual for Lawrence, who decided that on his return to England he would take Gardiner, not Hargrave, as his lieutenant. Looking to German youth for hope, and renting a house, they would start a "holy center" of leadership and "togetherness" from which they could emerge to save the English from socialism and democracy. What the workers of England needed,

25 *Die schöpferische Pause* (Jena, Diedrichs, 1921) by Fritz Klatt, who, during the 1920's, wrote several other books on the youth-movement and the plight of the spirit in the machine age.

said Lawrence, was not unions and strikes but folk songs and primitive dancing to the drum. Nothing came of these plans. In 1928 Lawrence sadly informed his friend that the modern world was no place for leadership, which had expired without trace in all but Gardiner, Mussolini, and Annie Besant.[26] But as *Apocalypse* shows, Lawrence never wholly abandoned his desire to lead the miners a song and dance.

It might be concluded from this that had Lawrence lived a few years longer he would have found the polity of his desire in Hitler's Germany. But there is every reason to doubt it. Lawrence wanted dictatorship, to be sure, but he was critical of every totalitarian system with which he was acquainted. For every favorable comment upon Mussolini and Italian fascism, Lawrence made several unfavorable comments. That stubborn individualism which made him incapable of deferring to the leadership of Mussolini, Lenin, or Hargrave would have kept him from welcoming Hitler. His reluctance to defer is to be seen in the conduct of Somers, the hero of *Kangaroo,* who faithfully reflects his creator. Weary of democracy and incapable of socialism, Somers is strongly attracted, as we have seen, to the fascism of Kangaroo. He feels lonely and disconnected, as every extreme individualist must, but his desire to join some authoritarian group is defeated by his own nature. "Somers would never be pals with any man," nor would he ever consent to be led. Though he talks of the need of authority and obedience, he prefers not to obey Kanga-

[26] *Letters,* pp. 604, 606, 666–67, 669, 671, 672–73, 675, 684, 695, 696, 697–700, 703, 704–5, 769.

roo.[27] Lawrence wanted tyranny on his own terms and only on condition that he be tyrant. It is in this way that he managed to reconcile his individualism, which had found itself so uneasy under democracy, with dictatorship. Throughout his life he dreamed of starting a community over which he could rule, and throughout his life this desire was frustrated by an individualism in others nearly as great as his own. It was only in the Utopia of Don Ramon, his Mexican dictator, that Lawrence's dreams found satisfaction. *The Plumed Serpent* represents his ideal state because he himself, under a splendid disguise, is dictator. Had Lawrence been able to get along with other men and had he possessed a capacity for leadership, he might have become a rival, not a follower, of Hitler, Mussolini, Hargrave, and Mosley—the boss of his private autocracy, like that romantic man the leader of P. G. Wodehouse's Black Shorts.

Lawrence differed in certain ways from these potential rivals. Like the Nazis he was anti-intellectual and primitivistic. But, more sentimental than any except the earliest of the Nazis, he wanted to destroy machines and money, not to control them. He desired a world without factories, capitalists, and proletariat, a world in which, as he called the turns, theosophists would dance tenderly about a sacred cow. His Utopia was patriarchal, like that, but on a grander scale, of Jack Grant, the hero of *The Boy in the Bush,* who retired to the wilderness with two wives and a horse. Lawrence was a religious man. He

27 *Kangaroo,* pp. 36, 115, and *passim;* cf. *Tales,* p. 613; *Phoenix,* p. 285; *Porcupine,* pp. 149–50.

wanted to be dictator; but he wanted to be high priest and prophet as well. His ideal of one or two in the bush is closer to the ideal of Moses or David or of the seventeenth-century theocrats, the Puritans of Massachusetts, for example, or of the Fifth Monarchy rebellions in England, than it is to that of the modern fascist. Hitler has not been immune from religious impulses and prophetical notions, but even Hitler appears worldly beside Lawrence. Hitler is a knave who uses religion to advance his secular ambitions. Lawrence was an enthusiast who wanted to use politics to advance his religion. It would be academic to deny this belated theocrat the label of proto-fascist to which he is entitled; but the interests of accuracy are better served by saying that Lawrence was a theocratic fascist.

The religious enthusiasm which distinguishes the Laurentian fascist may be observed in Rolf Gardiner, who, since his leader's death, has advocated a mixture of fascism and theocracy in a curious tract called *World without End, British Politics and the Younger Generation*, 1932.[28] For epigraph, Gardiner chose a passage concerning leadership from Lawrence's *Kangaroo*. And at the beginning of his text he confesses his debt to Lawrence, whose "pioneer work" has freed so many of Gardiner's generation from dead tradition, and "whose personal interest in, and criticism of, my activities were of ineffable and unforgettable worth." What every nation needs today, Gardiner continues, and this is the main

[28] Gardiner contributed an essay "*Die deutsche Revolution von England gesehen*" to *Nationalsozialismus vom Ausland gesehen* (Berlin, Verlag Die Runde, 1933), a collection of essays. In his essay Gardiner again quotes Lawrence with approval.

point of his tract, is some form of fascism. Surveying the varieties, he condemns Mosley's as too eclectic, Wyndham Lewis's as too odd, Mussolini's as too mechanical and worldly, and Hargrave's as too international. The National Socialists of Germany and D. H. Lawrence, however, have shown him the way to the proper kind. He recommends *The Plumed Serpent* as a guide for British fascists and Don Ramon as the pattern for the British leader. Combining the theocratic principles of Don Ramon with the practices of the Nazis, Gardiner proposes to make England what Lawrence called a "holy center" and from it with the aid of disciplined Nordics in other lands to lead Europe away from materialism, reason, liberalism, Russian atheism, and the Pope, back to adoration, obedience, and wordless mystery. But Gardiner is an imperfect Laurentian. In his Germanic theocracy he has failed to provide for the symbolical cow.

CHAPTER SEVEN

THE ARTIFICIAL ROCK

WHAT Susan meant to Lawrence and what place she held in that private religion she so conveniently symbolizes, though puzzling and seemingly unprofitable questions, should call no longer for conjecture. My quest of Susan through the depths of animism, theosophy, mindlessness, and the other matters religiously confounded by the bovolatrous man should not be unwelcome to those who like to explore the limits of contemporary thought. Some, however, while properly maintaining that elements and causes, to which I have devoted so much patience, are not the same as religions or religious novels, may pursue their distinction so far as to prefer not to know the origins of what they are fond, even when, or rather because, such knowledge makes plain the character, meaning, and value of the result. "Origins prove nothing," said William James. He meant, of course, that they are usually of less importance than what the creative imagination makes of them. Acquaintance, such as John Livingston Lowes has given us, with the raw materials of "The Ancient Mariner" serves only to emphasize the wonder of poetic creation. But when, as in the case of Lawrence, the creative imagination has failed to work its alchemy, the absurd raw materials, remaining raw and absurd, assume unusual importance. The meaning and value of the work remain the meaning and value of its materials, and some knowledge of them is necessary if the work is to be understood. Lawrence's religion and his novels are of most value, perhaps, to those who fail to understand them. Such people may be inclined to blame the investigator of origins, circumstances, and causes. But, as Alexander Pope said, "it is very unreasonable that people should expect us to be scholars and yet be angry to find us so."

Even to the most casual critic, Lawrence may seem a fool or a knave; but that he was not the latter is clear to anyone who is familiar with Lawrence's circumstances and with the origin and development of his beliefs. Sincere, sentimental, and, in the light of his aspirations, pathetic, Lawrence must seem another ineffectual angel. He was troubled, as many artists are, with nervous, physical, and social disadvantages, and he was aware of a world in confusion. His attempt to give meaning to the world or to make an adjustment between it and himself was of use only in showing that something was wrong, both with himself and with the world. Neurotic though it might be, his effort was less a symptom of his neurosis than a confused response to outer confusion. The additional symptoms of disorder which he spent his life in providing were unnecessary; but they are interesting to the historian in that Lawrence was as sensitive as any man to the disorder of the world and more sensitive than most to the current patterns of response. The patterns of his writhing, at once authentic and fashionable, make it easy to follow those of many other sensitive men and to understand the discomfort and behavior of the artist in modern times. Responding to the world about them in much the same way, many artists for the past one hundred and fifty years have been driven to the worship of something equivalent to the sacred cow. If Lawrence seems foolish in his devotion to an actual cow, not he nor she but their predecessors and the state of the world should be blamed.

In the Middle Ages the state of the world was bad, as every confessor knew, but since the Renaissance, according to many men of feeling, it has become increasingly worse. To such men, the improvements which modern times have brought to medicine, chemistry, and plumbing, for example, are of less consequence than the evils attending them. With every development of knowledge and of material convenience another spirit drooped, but however irrational these spirits were, they did not droop without reason; for the new age, though bringing almost as many evils as benefits, failed to take the place of what it had destroyed, and what was destroyed had conferred almost as many benefits as evils. During the sixteenth and seventeenth centuries, traditional certainties, which had comforted and inspired all men, were weakened by the attacks of humanists and Protestants. Aristotle retired under a cloud; the divided church lost authority; and the glory of God was somewhat impaired as man ascended the central throne. The social and economic order of the past broke first under mercantilism and then under industrial individualism. Men of the soil found themselves transplanted into cities, torn from what Mr. Eliot calls the roots that clutch and penetrate. Science, industry, and skeptical reason, the agents of change, made it difficult for many men to assent to former certainties, and no suitable equivalent was offered. By the nineteenth century, men of feeling found themselves in a world of individualism, change, and disorder, without a central belief to give it meaning, a world which appeared inimical to what they hopefully persisted in calling their souls.

The Augustan age in England was a time of reason and of humanistic order, or, at least, so it appeared to those who could not abide it. If there had been a church, the sensitive might have been contented; but, taking their character from the age, the surviving churches offered baroque interiors, elegant music, and reasonable doubts to those who could have been satisfied by nothing less than Bunyan, Wagner, and the Gothical. Some found what they wanted in Methodism, which appeared in response to their need with the enthusiasm of a lower class and of a less rational period. Others, who had become incapable of religion under its own name, took their spiritual recreation in sensibility and nature or in the exotic, the ancient, and the mysterious. Closing barren leaves, men of feeling incontinently retired to Gothic castles or to resorts more natural or more remote. At first the nineteenth century seemed congenial to those in retirement, but the plight of sensitive men soon became worse than that of their eighteenth-century predecessors as the higher critics and a new generation of rationalists and scientists began to remove what traditional supports remained. While Lyell, Chambers, Mill, and Colenso were pursuing reason, matter, and change, Tennyson confessed his agitation and doubt, and Arnold, infected with the strange disease of modern life, felt himself falling between two stools, one weak, the other waiting to be upholstered. Poets, painters, and composers came to hate the materialism and science which had deprived them of comfort and support. No longer satisfied with honest doubt, still less willing to adjust their emotions to the age, they took passionate flight from it into all that seemed opposite, into strange cults and mysteries, into philosophies of vitalism and flow, into primitivism, mythology, and nonsense. Bergson and Nietzsche, themselves in flight from logic and science, encouraged the artistic fugitives.

The relief such men demanded was still religious. Although they could not return to their former faith for the sake of enjoying the sentiment associated with it, the disillusioned were unable to dissociate emotion from belief. In this quandary, they often found the invention or the discovery of a substitute for the old belief to be inoffensive to their minds and pleasing to their sentiments. Science had not expelled religion but, driving it beneath the surface where it fretted for a time like a Freudian repression, had forced it to seek eccentric outlets and various disguises. The union of emotion and belief prospered in private.

Unhappy over Locke, Newton, and Voltaire and unable to find consolation in the faith of his fathers, William Blake assembled a private belief out of Swedenborg and Boehme and wrote its gospels. For the youthful Wordsworth and for Coleridge, Shelley, and Emerson, Platonism, German metaphysics, politics, or oriental mysticism provided very satisfactory substitutes for the established church. They and many of their equally

transcendental contemporaries lavished religious sentiments on objects which had been secular, such as birds
and flowers, for example, and music. To the reasonable
man of the preceding generation, music had been music, birds birds, and flowers flowers, and, however pleasing they may have been, they were nothing more. Now,
birds and flowers became sometimes the furniture of
private altars, sometimes the sacrifice, and music became
less the accompaniment than the way or even the object
of devotion. To Wagner and his congregation alike,
oboe calling to violin seemed to be deep calling unto
deep.

As the century declined, Darwin and his followers,
like Comus and his rout, had the odd effect of improv-
ing the piety of the pious. Although they made orthodoxy unacceptable to many as an outlet for religious
feeling, the evolutionists caused the orthodox to embrace the religion they professed and drove the disillusioned to further invention. Ruskin seems to have found
something equivalent to religion in a barbarous archi-
tecture, the Pre-Raphaelites found sanctuary in the Middle Ages, and the French symbolists discovered spiritual
relief from materialism in the vague, the suggestive, and
the mysterious. Samuel Butler's sentiments were chilled
by the scientific theories which had emancipated him
from the church. As emancipation ceased to entertain
him, his personal dislike of Darwin became religious intolerance, and Butler turned to Lamarck for a belief at
once acceptable to his mind and to his emotions. Although he continued for his own purposes to take facts
from Darwin, who did not understand their meaning,

Butler was less interested in facts than in hope. During the intervals when he was not distracted by Pauli or Jones, Butler worshiped the life-force in a private shrine and devoted his pen to religious controversy so much like that of the seventeenth century that only the simple could be deceived by his substitution of vitalism for dipping and of science for the Whore of Babylon. He destroyed Darwin; he destroyed Huxley's foolish theory about protoplasm; he wrote: "Will the reader bid me wake with him to a world of chance and blindness? Or can I persuade him to dream with me of a more living faith than either he or I had as yet conceived possible? . . . faith and hope . . . beckon to the dream." [1] What he wrote cannot be called art; but for many of those who were capable of it, art became, as in the age of Shelley, the medium for religion. Bernard Shaw, for example, much brighter and much more the artist than Samuel Butler, was even more religious. His hard brilliance concealed a tender spirit which felt cramped by the age of Darwin. Prevented by the fashion of skepticism from embracing the Church of England or even Methodism, he proclaimed his hatred of science, especially of medicine and natural selection, and devised a private and eclectic belief to satisfy his sentiments, which found expression and relief in socialism, Wagner, Nietzsche, Butler, Bunyan, Bergson, and the spiritual vegetarianism of Shelley. Shaw's enthusiasm sublimated secular objects like socialism, which were disarmingly agreeable to his intellect. Wagner, Butler, Nietzsche, and Bergson were already so transcendental as to require

[1] *Life and Habit* (London, Cape, 1923), p. 250.

nothing further to be pleasing and so up-to-date as not only to flatter his intellect into suspension of disbelief but to secure its aid. The deep of Wagner called unto the deep of the perfect Wagnerite, who devoted many of his plays and other tracts to sermons on his transcendental experience. Like so much of the literature since Darwin, Shaw's plays form the gospels of a singular religion. Indeed, he compared *Man and Superman* to the spiritual works of Wagner and Shelley and described this play as a religious manual, a bible for evolutionists, not, of course, for Darwinians but for the followers of Samuel Butler, who made a religion of science.[2] Even H. G. Wells, whose nature is much less ethereal than Shaw's, was driven to describe as bibles the works which he devotes to the salvation of mankind.[3] Aldous Huxley's youthful irony and despair over the miserable condition of humanity were succeeded first by his tentative discipleship to D. H. Lawrence [4] and then by a

[2] Preface, *Man and Superman*. This Preface, in which Shaw describes his conscience as the "genuine pulpit article," is important for understanding the character of contemporary literature. He calls *Back to Methuselah* a pentateuch and describes one of his recent plays as an apocalypse. In the Preface to *Back to Methuselah*, Shaw calls for a religious revival against materialism, not a retreat to orthodoxy but a new vitalist religion with himself as prophet. He awaits disciples. To those who complained about his apparent levity, Shaw once said the real joke was that he was "in earnest."

In *The Devil's Disciple*, he shows how the really religious man, like Prometheus, Siegfried, or Dick Dudgeon, is forced by his inability to accept conventional religion into inventing a religion of his own. The Philistine doctor in *The Doctor's Dilemma* who thinks Shaw is a Methodist preacher is not so far wrong as Shaw seems to have thought.

[3] Preface, *The Open Conspiracy* (1928): "This is, I declare, the truth and the way of salvation." Wells's religion of humanity is similar to that of Comte.

[4] See John H. Roberts, "Huxley and Lawrence," *The Virginia Quarterly Review*, XIII (1937), 546–57.

tentative religion of his own, which he preaches in essay and novel. The communism or fascism of some of the more, as well as some of the less, literate advocates of these cures for what ails us has the appearance of religion rather than of politics or economics. And Kipling's imperial enthusiasm, which in another age might have been no more than imperial, was imperfectly secular.

In the words of William Butler Yeats, written during the late nineties but as true today, the arts are foreshadowing "the new sacred book." "How can the arts," he asked, "overcome the slow dying of men's hearts that we call the progress of the world, and lay their hands upon men's heart-strings again, without becoming the garment of religion as in old times?" All over Europe, he said, writers and painters, dissatisfied with materialism and externality, are "beginning to be interested in many things which positive science, the interpreter of exterior law, has always denied. . . . We are about to substitute once more the distillations of alchemy for the analyses of chemistry . . ." Yeats saw hopeful signs of this substitution in the work of Blake, Wagner, Maeterlinck, and Villiers de l'Isle-Adam, who had assumed the task once performed by orthodox religion: "The arts are, I believe, about to take upon their shoulders the burdens that have fallen from the shoulders of priests . . ." [5] The poet as prophet and priest is a notion by no means original. Plato maintained it, and after the revival of learning, Spenser and Milton too. Since their time, however, the growth of materialism and

[5] "The Autumn of the Body," "Symbolism in Painting," "The Symbolism of Poetry," in *Essays* (New York, Macmillan, 1924), pp. 200, 235, 237; cf. pp. 184, 190–91.

disorder and the decline of established religions have given the Platonic notion new point and increasing currency. That Yeats and so many of his contemporaries fell heir to the prophetical sensations and robes of Blake, Shelley, and Wagner is the most natural thing in the world.

Should Dante descend to the present with Mr. Eliot as guide, he could not easily believe that our age had undone so many. Nor could he observe without pity and fear that what has driven so many to eccentric religions has burdened the more reasonable artist with a sense of isolation and discomfort. In a world without such traditions and beliefs as he can hang his feelings on, the least transcendental artist, while hunting for some convenient order, may suitably lament his lot. His position is that of James Joyce's Stephen Dedalus, who isolated himself from father, country, and religion. But what has been forced upon others to the detriment of their art, Stephen deliberately achieved for the sake of his. The aesthetic order created by this exile to take the place of another order which could no longer support him was insufficient, however, to repair his sense of loss. The want of father, country, and religion remained to plague him; and Stephen's symbolic hunt for a father became the theme of *Ulysses*. This hunt for a father, for something to replace Dante's God, is the pursuit of the contemporary artist. That it should end so often with Mr. Bloom is a great pity, but his value as a symbol is plain, as Thomas Wolfe perceived. Crying "O lost!" he joined the symbolic chase, and the significance of the quarry seemed to him to justify the lengths to which the hunter might go. Critics who complained that the lengths to which Wolfe went were a vengeance for the loss of his father more terrible than Donna Anna's for the loss of hers appear to have forgotten the necessity of the hunt, about which Wolfe said:

. . . the deepest search in life, it seemed to me, the one thing that in one way or another was central to all living was man's search to find a father, not merely the father of his flesh, not merely the lost father of his youth, but the image of a strength and wisdom external to his need and superior to his hunger, to which the belief and power of his own life could be united.[6]

Under a different metaphor, T. S. Eliot sought similar refuge from this his exile. Before he came upon a metaphor, he imagined he had found his peace in the secular traditions of the past, especially the great tradition of European letters. He thought he could find a private center in Donne, Laforgue, Webster, and Marvell. But although the secular past had power to center his art, it failed to satisfy his sentiments, and, finding his metaphor, he began to wander in the Waste Land of the present, where the traditions he had relied upon had the appearance of fossil remains. If only there were water and no rocks, he was saying, when among the fossils he beheld the Rock, somewhat decayed, perhaps, and less awful than it had been, but solid enough for him.[7] Unlike the spiritual orphans who were not so easily appeased, Eliot had found asylum in what remained of a past belief, as the Tractarians, Oscar Wilde, and Ches-

[6] *The Story of a Novel* (New York, Scribner's, 1936), p. 39.
[7] See also Eliot's poem about the little dog who finds shelter from the Waste Land under a cretonne comforter: *Collected Poems, 1909–1935* (New York, Harcourt, Brace, 1936), p. 167.

terton had done before him. Such refuge may strike some as being, in our day, little better than the eccentric religions of those who could not accept the conventional.[8] Some may put Eliot down for a fool or a knave; but that he is not the former is clear from the observation of one of the characters in his "Dialogue on Dramatic Poetry" to the effect that our literature has become a substitute for religion, and so has our religion.[9]

Lawrence was as certain as Eliot that belief is necessary for art.[10] Echoing Eliot and Lawrence in their demand for a Rock, Somers of *Kangaroo* asked: " 'Where is my Rock of Ages?' " [11] Lawrence differed from Eliot, however, in refusing to be contented with a ready-made refuge. After the manner of Blake, Shelley, Yeats, Shaw, and the other prophets, Lawrence privately invented a substitute for the Rock, an artificial rock, which was to him what the Church of England is to Eliot. As the cross symbolically adorns Eliot's Rock, so Susan symbolically presided over Lawrence's geological invention.

From his Rock, Eliot was compelled to contemplate a Waste Land disfigured by artificial rocks in great numbers; for the erection of these monuments had become the principal diversion of romantics. The substitute or private religion, which I have been pursuing, may be described with greater historical point as the central

8 "The view that what we need in this tempestuous turmoil of change is a Rock to shelter under or to cling to, rather than an efficient aeroplane in which to ride it, is comprehensible but mistaken." I. A. Richards, *Principles of Literary Criticism* (New York, Harcourt, Brace, 1934), p. 57.

9 *Selected Essays* (New York, Harcourt, Brace, 1934), p. 32. This epigram is patterned on Oscar Wilde's epigram on Meredith and Browning.

10 *Fantasia*, p. 11; *Letters*, p. 688.   11 *Kangaroo*, p. 314.

element of the recent romantic movement. Romantic and romanticism are tiresome labels, perhaps better left alone, but of some use when narrowly limited and applied to the art of the last one hundred and fifty years as aids to the understanding of its character.[12] Romanticism has been described as the return to nature and as nostalgia for the remote in time or place; it has been said to involve wonder, strangeness, imagination, mysticism, unreason, or even sickness and perversity. The variety of its aspects led Professor Lovejoy to refer not to romanticism but to romanticisms.[13] Professor Fairchild, however, so defined the term as to reconcile the aspects:

Romanticism is the endeavor, in the face of growing factual obstacles, to achieve, to retain, or to justify that illusioned view of the universe and of human life which is produced by an imaginative fusion of the familiar and the strange, the known and the unknown, the real and the ideal, the finite and the infinite, the material and the spiritual, the natural and the supernatural.[14]

He noted that, during the early nineteenth century, emphasis began to fall less upon the actual in this fusion than upon the transcendental. His study does not deal, save for some forward glances, with the development of romanticism after Wordsworth and Shelley, but it is clear that the transcendental element has persisted. Nature and the past have excited new illusions, and the

[12] See Mario Praz, Introduction, *The Romantic Agony* (London, Oxford University Press, 1933).

[13] A. O. Lovejoy, "On the Discrimination of Romanticisms," *Publication of the Modern Language Association*, XXXIX, 229–53.

[14] *The Romantic Quest* (New York, Columbia University Press, 1931), p. 251; cf. pp. 146–47, 246–52.

most unlikely things, such as vegetables, politics, animals, unintelligence, and music, have retained, increased, or acquired religious significance. So religious, indeed so evangelical [15] its character that, if we take Alexander Pope's phrase in a Wesleyan rather than in the Augustan sense, post-Wordsworthian romanticism may be defined as nature methodized. T. E. Hulme, who complained that humanism was a confusion between the human and the divine and who saw romanticism as the degenerate product of this confusion, called romanticism "spilt religion." [16] His definition is apt, if we limit it to nineteenth- and twentieth-century developments; for, although romanticism has retained some secular features and accompaniments, it has generally assumed the shape of the bootleg or substitute religion, the cult of the artificial rock. In this shape it has become the religion of the machine age. And in view of the number of literary prophets and priests who have celebrated its rites upon synthetic altars, the romantic in our day might better be called the mantic.

There is a common idea, inspired perhaps by textbooks on literature, that romanticism softly and suddenly vanished away in 1837 or thereabouts, that the Victorian period was essentially different from its predecessor, and that with the arrival of the twentieth century or with the war came a new dispensation. However attractive this idea may be to those who prefer Venetian blinds and tubular furniture to lace curtains and anti-

[15] See G. M. Young, *Victorian England* (Oxford, Oxford University Press, 1936), pp. 1–3, for the pervasiveness of the evangelical temper.

[16] T. E. Hulme, *Speculations* (New York, Harcourt, Brace, 1924), pp. 48, 56, 61, 118.

macassars, it is not sound. We are still in the age of
Rousseau and Wordsworth and are likely to continue so
for some time longer. We are belated, perhaps decadent,
romantics. It is possible, of course, to distinguish ourselves and our times by other names, but no better purpose is served by critics who call the present a period
of transition, for example, than by historians who an-
nounce that at such and such a time the middle classes
were emerging. Every age is an age of transition and the
middle classes are always emerging. Change is natural
within any historical period, so that our time appears
to be and is somewhat different, on the surface at least,
from Wordsworth's, but it is essentially similar.

We have seen that in the time of Wordsworth romanticism was the sensitive man's response to the Augustan tradition, that before having had time to expire
of prosperity and excess the romantic movement took
a new lease on life from Darwin and those dogmatic
empiricists who were his followers, and that the Victorian revival of the romantic, like its eighteenth-century
origin, was a symptom that man's emotions had failed
to keep up with his rational and material development.
Although it became less dogmatic with the years, science,
which caused the revival of romanticism, has been
largely responsible for its continuation. As the new
physics soared above logic, some scientists like Edding-
ton, however, have soared with it to the metaphysical;
for, as Professor William Montague has observed, the
new mathematical universe curves around in such a
manner as not only to defy the understanding but so as
to leave a convenient place in the middle for a god.

The mysteries revealed by the psychoanalysts have been equally agreeable to those in rebellion against the behaviorists, who seemed to be occupied with nothing more spiritual than pulling habits out of rats. But on the whole, although the recent developments of science may seem more congenial, science and the scientist remain as hostile and repulsive as ever to the lover of the ineffable. The scientist may confess ignorance or reveal mysteries, but he requires evidence for what he believes and does not adore what he does not know. Romantics feel blighted and confined, in our day as earlier, by such factual austerity.[17] Demanding why and not how, they still pursue their attempt to say what cannot be said.

Disorder as well as science has promoted the persistence of the romantic attitude. The want of a central belief, the specialization which has broken the bond of common knowledge, the complexity of science which discourages all but the specialist, and our social and economic troubles have fostered singular retreats. It would be surprising and unnatural if this age of science and disorder had produced a classical literature.

In our time, romanticism has taken two principal forms, both religious. The first is the discovery of a sentimental refuge in a past or future order, through which the disorder or materialism of the present may be escaped. Many reasonable men, who are trying to cure the evils of the present, might appear to be included in this category; but the words *sentimental* and *escape* are intended to prevent their inclusion. On the other hand, many converts to communism or to the

[17] Cf. Fairchild, *Romantic Quest,* pp. 254–56.

established religions deserve to be included, but their romantic refuge in an established belief is less romantic than that of the solitary refugee. The second form of current romanticism is making a religion out of disorder and worshiping flux, mystery, or feeble-mindedness. Although they display different degrees of piety and certain alien qualities, Bergson, Virginia Woolf, Herbert Read, and the surrealists belong in this class. Some contemporary writers, like Yeats and Shaw, manage to combine both forms of romanticism and not infrequently to add reasonable elements to the combination without regard for consistency.

This should surprise no one; for we are not confronted with a question of French literature, in which divisions are said to be exact, but of English, which has always been like Sir Thomas Browne's Griffin, a mixed and dubious animal, having fore parts of one sort and hind parts of another. In the most classical age of England, romantic elements were present; since something like the romantic habit of mind is normal in that country. And in the most romantic times, such as the early nineteenth century, people as unromantic as Jane Austen appear. The present is no exception to this want of rule. Although the period is generally romantic, some authors are far less romantic than others and some show only certain external characteristics of the distemper. Arnold Bennett, for example, was without the slightest inclination toward the transcendental. Much more romantic than Bennett, H. G. Wells, who produces bibles, projects visions of the future, and expects too much of science, calls himself a scientific materialist. Much more romantic than Wells, Virginia Woolf, whose work deals with intuition, flux, and what she calls soul, has a very pretty wit. And not a few recent authors, such as George Moore and Edith Sitwell, have possessed the fashionable accompaniments or externals of the romantic without a trace of the religious spirit which produced them. Perhaps the least romantic writers of our day are those who, although using romantic materials and techniques, keep the artist's distance from his materials and refuse to merge themselves mystically with what they use. Henry James, Lytton Strachey, and T. S. Eliot (in spite of his Rock) are of this extraordinary company. It is worth noting that James Joyce, perhaps the best of the lot, did not take the rocky road from Dublin.

To be sure, there are certain men, including Eliot, who like to call themselves classicists. Conspicuous among these are the Humanists, the Neo-Thomists of France, the Anglo-American followers of T. E. Hulme, and the Aristotelians of the Middle West. Their common bond seems to be a dislike of the word romantic, which, as often as they have the chance, they contemptuously reject. For many years, however, the word has been of ill repute in certain romantic quarters. Shaw saved it for his worst enemies; and Irving Babbitt made it equivalent to the source of all evil. The followers of Hulme, such as Eliot, Wyndham Lewis, and Herbert Read, appear to be fascinated with the detestable word. After defiantly calling himself a classicist in literature, as well as a Royalist in politics and an Anglo-Catholic in religion, T. S. Eliot thought better of it and suppressed the label, wisely concluding that the classic is an ideal which in our romantic day can be realized only "in tendency." [18]

This nostalgia for the classical, as of the moth for the star, is perhaps the best evidence of our romanticism. In a classical period, a man does not have to go about proclaiming his classicism; nor, supposing him capable of such a proclamation, does he proceed, with Stephen Leacock's romantic hero, to dash madly off in all directions. Self-labeled classicists, ambiguously existing in our time, cannot escape its consequences, and their ideal is but another romantic retreat, little different from the private religions they deplore. Of course, if every age is an age of transition and if the elements of coming times are always concealed in the present, the romantic classicists of today may be heralds sad and trumpets of a classical future.

While we impatiently await, or labor to postpone, this classical future, in which literature, perhaps, will have adjusted itself to fact, it is fitting that we should understand the unclassical present. For this purpose D. H. Lawrence is very useful. In his life and work he conveniently combined most of the elements of contemporary romanticism. In his transcendental attitude toward nature, savages, the past, intuition, and the relations between men and women and in his devotion to Susan, the central religious tendency of recent romanticism is plain. His more than Methodist enthusiasm, his sensibility, his sensationalism, and his hatred of science and reason are the normal accompaniments or manifestations of the

[18] Preface, *For Lancelot Andrewes* (London, Faber & Gwyer, 1928); *Selected Essays*, pp. 15–18, 340; *After Strange Gods*, pp. 26–31, 37.

modern distemper. His sufferings and response were those of the sentimental artist in our times. It is true that Lawrence was completer and more extreme than most of his contemporaries, but for this reason he is a more suitable subject for study; for the extreme, as every schoolteacher knows, is the easiest approach to the normal. As Lawrence's times, contemporaries, and predecessors account for the way in which his neurotic sensibility responded, so Lawrence affords one of the best approaches to the understanding of his times, contemporaries, and predecessors. And through Susan, the typical romantic object, lies the readiest approach to the character of much of our literature and religion.

The religious impulse, which used to be the nurse or friend of art, has become more or less its enemy. In Dante's time the artist, whether an architect, a sculptor, or a poet, found in his faith a center for his emotions, the stimulation he required, and a common store of images. Under an accepted belief, work of the most didactic intention may possess aesthetic interest; even the sermons, allegories, and cautionary tales which rely upon an external value may acquire a value of their own. T. S. Eliot has said, and there is no reason to quarrel with him about it, that dependence upon a received tradition, especially a religious one, is good for art. But in our day, when few precedents are left to broaden down from and those that do remain are often found to be unacceptable, the artist, as we have seen, is sometimes driven to invention. The effect of the private religion upon art, especially upon Lawrence's, has been unfortunate. But before such a generalization may be made, or, at least, received, we must consider Lawrence's art, noting what he is good at and at what he is bad.

Lawrence the novelist, for I shall not touch upon his verse, was very good at what he knew or saw—the miners, for example, and the pits, engines, and haystacks of his native district. These he had made his own before he matured, and the short stories or the novels, such as *Sons and Lovers,* for which he drew upon the experiences of his youth are effective in so far as he did not stray from them. Throughout his life he retained a peculiar sensitivity to what he called the spirit of place. With Thomas Hardy, whom he imitated when he first began to write, Lawrence had the ability to seize upon and convey the feeling of localities, whether of the Nottingham district as at first or later of more exotic places such as Italy, Australia, and Mexico. Perhaps the chief merit of *The Plumed Serpent* is the strangeness and intensity of the Mexico which Lawrence saw as nobody else had seen. The lights he saw upon the mountains of America or upon the coasts of Australia may have never been on land or sea, but, glowing intensely where his imagination projected them, they have become real for others. Whatever else they may lack, Lawrence's novels and essays are the best travelogues of our day. The creatures with which he peopled the places of his visits are not as convincing or as well-conceived as their environment, but their relationships with each other are independently alive. Lawrence could convey to the least intuitive reader a sense of the subtle awareness vibrating between Somers of *Kangaroo* and those around him, the all but ineffable knowledge floating between two cats in

Women in Love, and the strange, half-conscious connection between Ursula and the horses in *The Rainbow* or, in its sequel, between Gudrun and the cow, when she danced before cows. He enlarged the novel's field of sensitivity to include levels below those explored by Henry James or James Joyce, who had penetrated the flow of awareness before him.[19] Woman confronting woman may enjoy the almost bestial intuitions in which he dealt, but no woman writer, not even Mrs. Woolf, has successfully recorded them, perhaps because no woman writer has been at once as feminine and as gifted as he. No one in our day has approached him in his ability to translate experience into fantasy, sometimes with the aid of ancient myths and generally with their hypnotic effect. At its best, the prose he devised to express his intuitions is suitable. With its rhythm, redundancy, and mantic overtones, it has the power of the tom-tom to provoke emotions and to dull the mind.

Despite such merits, D. H. Lawrence never wrote a first-rate novel. It is a pity that no sooner had he commenced writing than he began to depart from what he knew or saw to what he thought he knew. A process like that which made his landscapes fabulous all but spoiled the characters of his fiction. Instead of projecting a light, he projected a theory which distorted or impaired the evidence of his senses. Like the characters in a bad allegory or in a melodrama, his characters, who also served to point attitudes toward life, rarely achieve a life of their own. Theory and purpose prevented Lawrence

[19] Cf. I. A. Richards, *On Imagination* (New York, Harcourt, Brace, 1935), pp. 220–25.

not only from seeing what was there to see but from creating a reality independent of the actual. In one of his essays T. S. Eliot says that Thomas Hardy, though neither a Dryden nor a Dante, sacrificed his philosophy to vision and apprehended his materials as a poet should.[20] Lawrence conspicuously failed to do this. His Birkins, Ciprianos, Ursulas, and gamekeepers are incompletely realized. They are creatures not of imagination but of logic. Wandering through intense landscapes, they utter improbable sermons while their improbable actions illustrate good or evil. When his heroes are not preaching, Lawrence is. The characters of *Pilgrim's Progress,* the greatest work with which Lawrence's novels have much in common, are better realized, and the didacticism behind them is less oppressive; for when he felt like preaching, Bunyan could deliver a sermon in his meetinghouse. Lawrence had no recourse but to write another novel.

Lawrence shared with Bunyan the idea that art without a philosophy and a didactic purpose is of little worth. This opinion is not necessarily inimical to art; many people, like Bunyan, have produced art while intending to instruct. What is more, art dependent upon a theory may be good even if the theory is no longer acceptable. One's enjoyment of a stained-glass window is not dependent upon acceptance of the theory or purpose behind the glass. If theory had interfered with art by making the glass opaque, one might reasonably quarrel with both theory and art. But the theory behind medieval

[20] "The Possibility of a Poetic Drama," *The Sacred Wood* (London, Methuen, 1928), p. 66.

glass was so clear to the artist and so completely felt that it could be objectified in something with an existence independent of artist and belief. Lawrence's ideas were confused; they were never completely objectified; and they interfered continually with his art.

The ideas or sense of a literary work, as I. A. Richards has shown, may affect its aesthetic value. What he says appears to be true in that it is harder to suspend the reader's disbelief and enlist his imagination if his response is divided by critical disagreement. Work depending upon ideas which have been incompletely realized and objectified may perish with these ideas when they have been outmoded or when they have been shown to be nonsense. The first is the fate of Shaw's early plays, the second of Lawrence's novels. Some apprehension of the danger which Lawrence was incurring may have moved George Moore to advise the young poet to return to his dahlias and to forsake vague sensual abstractions.[21]

Lawrence could never keep his eye on the dahlia. It is true that he once said: "Life and love are life and love, a bunch of violets is a bunch of violets, and to drag in the idea of a point is to ruin everything." [22] But such moments of clarity were rare, and, commonly, no sooner had he taken up his pen than violet and dahlia were sublimated to an unbotanical plane where they lay, covered with confusion. Here they could keep abstract company with life and love, which had also been at-

[21] Joseph Hone, *The Life of George Moore*, p. 347.

[22] *Assorted Articles*, p. 49. Lawrence's poems on birds, beasts, and flowers, for example, show his tendency to stray from the object to the lessons it suggests. His poem "Figs" is a medieval exemplum, a sermon with the fruit as text. Cf. "Tortoise Shell," *Collected Poems*, II, 129, 133, 224, 274.

tended to by the poet. Lawrence's vague transcendentalism and inner confusion may have made the natural
sublime, but they were of little help in creating an
aesthetic order out of the materials of nature.

If his work is to have form or order a writer, even a
novelist, must have inner unity, especially in times of
outer confusion like the present. To be sure, many novels of more orderly days have been formless, and the
novel has never developed a form as tight as that of the
drama. But following the necessities of its nature and
reflecting the internal unity of the more fortunate novelists, even in our day the novel has found an appropriate form. The novels of Henry James, who was conscious
of the disorder and decay around him, provided formal
antidotes to the times they ironically depicted.[23] *Ulysses,*
which is perhaps the most intricate literary structure
since *The Divine Comedy,* reveals Joyce's ideal of the
formal relation of part to part for an aesthetic end and
possesses that wholeness, harmony, and radiance which
Aquinas found essential to the work of art.[24] Even the
novels of Virginia Woolf have a formal rhythm which
her adherence to the Bergsonian theory of art seems
scarcely to have impaired. Sharing her aesthetic convictions and revealing his own disorder, D. H. Lawrence
thought order to be so alien to life that he could conceive of it only as something imposed from without to
his soul's impediment. Despite this conviction, however, he appears to have made some attempt to give order

[23] See Henry James's dismissal of Lawrence on aesthetic grounds in
Notes on Novelists, pp. 321–44.

[24] See James Joyce, *A Portrait of the Artist as a Young Man* (New
York, Huebsch, 1916), pp. 240–51.

to his books by following the pattern of familiar myths as Joyce did in *Ulysses* and Eliot in *The Waste Land.*[25] But his contempt of form and his conviction that truth is enough for beauty prevented Lawrence from making the most of such mythical scaffolds. His use of myth was too desultory to repel confusion. Most of his novels remain without the wholeness and harmony which would make them art; and such radiance as they possess is not from the novels themselves but from their landscapes.

A capacity which under happier circumstances might have produced good novels produced instead queer allegories, some of which, like *Kangaroo, Lady Chatterley,* and *Aaron's Rod,* are all but unreadable, others of which, like *Women in Love, The Rainbow,* or *The Boy in the Bush,* conceal excellent passages in mazes of tedious didacticism.[26] *Sons and Lovers* and *The Plumed Serpent,* however, are works in which Lawrence's capacity somehow struggled through obstacles placed in its way by nature and circumstance. The strange splendor of his Mexican fantasy makes its faults seem inconspicuous. In the cult of Quetzalcoatl, Lawrence found at last what T. S. Eliot has called an "objective correlative," and the result of this discovery approached art if not sense. Moreover, it cannot be denied that several of

[25] See "Lawrence and the Myth," unpublished Columbia M.A. thesis, 1938, by Irwin Swerdlow, one of my students, who has made a thorough and original study of Lawrence's use of Genesis and of Wagner in his novels. Mr. Swerdlow's conclusions, however, are more favorable to Lawrence than mine. See also T. S. Eliot, "Ulysses, Order, and Myth," *The Dial,* LXXV (November, 1923), 480–83.

[26] Although *The Lost Girl* is relatively free from any but implicit preaching, it is a feeble novel except at the beginning and at the end, the first part resembling Arnold Bennett, the last representing Lawrence at his best. This book appears to have been an effort to conciliate hostile publishers and public. Of *The Trespasser* the less said the better.

Lawrence's short stories, especially "The Man Who Died," have merit; nor can it be denied that his familiar letters are suitably familiar. But these are exceptions, and his typical work is neither a rearrangement of the actual like *Sons and Lovers* nor a fantasy like *The Plumed Serpent* but something between a sermon and a fairy tale without the virtues of either kind.

The defects of Lawrence's novels may be traced to his private religion. His attempt to combine the functions of prophet, priest, and artist was too ambitious for his capacity. Even an orthodox priest, who does not pretend to be an artist, would find it less difficult to become one; for he is not under the necessity of establishing the religion he preaches. The anxiety of the private priest not only to promote but to formulate his creed leaves him with a less than priestly chance to cultivate sensory and formal interests. What is more, he suffers from a disadvantage not shared by orthodox priest or communicant; because of an undisciplined confusion of the natural with the divine, the religious interest taken by the private priest in what must constitute the materials of art prevents that detachment from them which is necessary for art.[27] More eager to explain than to arrange the natural and distracted by internal division, he is unable to keep his eye on the dahlia, from which the priest's might soar with less damage than the artist's.

Lawrence's art suffered more than that of others from the religious dilemma of recent times, but it did not suffer alone. Shaw's plays, as I have said, reveal similar

[27] See Julien Benda, *Belphegor* (London, Faber & Faber, 1929), for the tendency of recent artists to merge mystically with their materials.

effects of the same cause. Without the time or temper to dramatize his prophetical notions, Shaw placed them in the mouths of dummies seated about a succession of round tables. For his purposes, as he seems to have realized, the preface, or even the appendix, was a more congenial medium than the play, in which his religious impulse and his dramatic talent could only quarrel. If it is true that Shaw knows the truth, his plays, as he himself has implied, are too true to be good; but it is a pity that he did not devote his critical gifts to something more important than anticipating his critics. The poems of A.E. and the essays of Herbert Read are ghostly substitutes for what they appear to be. The writings of H. G. Wells, Virginia Woolf, and the later Aldous Huxley are more successful in that they are less privately sublime. Alone of those who have cultivated a private belief, William Butler Yeats escaped its usual effects; for he alone had critical detachment. He knew that he needed the stimulation of faith for his art and that for him the private religion was all that our times afforded. But he also saw that his art must not explicitly express the system upon which it depended. Aware of the dangers of sentimentality and abstraction which confront the private priest, although succumbing at times to one or the other, as in his early poems or in "The Phases of the Moon," he consciously purged himself of both, leaving his poetry free to be poetry. A union of critical intelligence and superior genius saved him from the fate of Lawrence and Shaw and allowed him to enjoy the benefits of a private faith without its dangers.

His compatriot James Joyce is extraordinary in being

able to dispense with the stimulation of belief. After his abandonment of revealed religion, Joyce was preserved from the need of a substitute by his self-sufficiency [28] and by the effects of a religion in which he no longer believed. The Jesuitical discipline of Aristotle and Aquinas, directed to secular and aesthetic ends, helped his art to steer Mr. Bloom's course between the rock of dogma and the whirlpool of mysticism,[29] while, without such aids to navigation and imperfectly cradled in the deep, Lawrence's art was wrecked upon the artificial rock.

Although the Anglo-Catholicism of T. S. Eliot is parallel in certain ways to the private religion, it has left his art intact; for the Church of England maintains a salaried priesthood and its creed has been more or less established. Exempted from preaching in his poetry, Eliot may moralize with impunity in his prose. In *After Strange Gods,* for example, he draws lessons from the arts of an age without a living and central tradition, an age, as he correctly describes it, of messianic impulse, inner light, and individual religions. He attributes the health and integrity of Joyce's art and the sickness of Lawrence's to the effects on the one hand of orthodoxy and on the other of heresy.[30] Whatever the implication of these terms to Eliot, he is right on purely aesthetic grounds in ascribing virtues to the orthodox and evils to the heterodox or what I have called the private religion; but he ignores the possibility that irreligion,

[28] In Stephen's hunt for a father, Joyce seems to have symbolized less his own necessity than that of most contemporary artists.

[29] See the Scylla and Charybdis episode in *Ulysses.*

[30] *After Strange Gods,* pp. 41, 48, 53, 63–66.

like that of Henry James, Arnold Bennett, and Lytton Strachey, may be as good for art as orthodoxy, or, as I. A. Richards has suggested, even better. Indeed, this belated nineteenth-century materialist sees hope for art only after the emotions shall have been separated from their dependence upon belief.[31] However fond this hope may appear in our romantic time, one may share his conviction that on the whole it would be better for art if religion were kept in church where it can do no harm.

There is much to learn from Lawrence, said Mr. Eliot, but, he added, those who have the judgment to draw a lesson are not those who have need of it. He fears that Lawrence's work appeals not to the discriminating reader but to the unhealthy and the confused.[32] Crying *woe unto the foolish prophets, that follow their own spirit, and have seen nothing,* and with other pious ejaculations, Eliot proceeds to draw a lesson for which he has the necessary judgment. What he says about Lawrence's audience or, better, about his cult is perfectly sound. To the accompaniment of shrill cries from classicists, humanists, and moralists, and followed by the concern of reasonable men, this cult has flourished and expanded until it includes not only communists, fascists, and literary critics but innumerable women and ambiguous creatures. Lawrence wanted art, and what he

[31] *Science and Poetry,* especially Chapter VI, "Poetry and Beliefs," and Chapter VII, "Some Contemporary Poets." The latter chapter contains excellent criticism of Yeats and Lawrence.

[32] *After Strange Gods,* pp. 66–67. Cf. Eliot's review of Murry's *Son of Woman* in *The Criterion,* X (July, 1931), 768–74. Mr. Eliot's observations about this audience are confirmed by the organ of the Lawrence cult: *The Phoenix, a Quarterly.* See in particular Vol. I, No. 2 (June–August, 1938), pp. 129–30, in which the editor hails Lawrence as the saviour and his primitivism and mindlessness as the truth and the way.

said was generally foolish; but he has not wanted devotion.

Many have found his ideas attractive; for Lawrence was so much the man of his time as to have expressed the preoccupations of the postwar world or at least of its more modish levels. To the sophisticated his hatred of democracy, his interest in dictators, and his concern with anthropology, flux, the unconscious, and love were irresistible. Others who remain more or less indifferent to his ideas admire him for the emotion with which he expressed them. It is for this reason, apparently, that recent critics in *The Times Literary Supplement* have proclaimed Lawrence *"the* genius of our time." [33] W. H. Auden speaks with some tenderness of Lawrence's "wonderful wooziness," [34] forgetting, perhaps, that the expression of feeling in itself is of little worth and that however wonderful wooziness may be it is still wooziness. Others admire in Lawrence a certain urgency or vitality, forgetting that vitality alone, like the spinach to which it is commonly attributed, is not enough.

The important cause of Lawrence's vogue, even among those who may appear to fancy his ideas, is his tone. By his enthusiasm, depth, and solemnity Lawrence gives many people of our times the emotional relief they need in such times, and by his vague yearning he expresses theirs. Those to whom Wagner seems profound have discovered in Lawrence their perfect expression.

[33] January 8 and June 18, 1938.
[34] W. H. Auden and Louis Macneice, *Letters from Iceland* (New York, Random House, 1937), pp. 210, 221. Cf. Auden, *Poems* (New York, Random House, 1934), p. 41, where Lawrence, William Blake, and Homer Lane are seen as "healers" of the world's distempers.

He was a Father Divine for the literate. Their interest in him is less literary than religious, whatever its disguise. They do not understand what he meant, so they feel that it is deep. His success makes it plain that to please such people it is not enough to be foolish; one must also be solemn.

Julien Benda has described in *Belphegor* the demand of this audience for emotion, mystical merging, and flow and its hatred of outline, detachment, and wit. John Strachey, a communist who has little affection for Lawrence, has noted the yearning of this audience for emotional metaphysics.[35] This taste, which he ascribes to bourgeois decadence, was ascribed by T. E. Hulme to the persistence of romanticism. I prefer the latter explanation. Lawrence's audience is as romantic as he was, and the appearance of his cult is but another symptom of the temper of the times.

[35] John Strachey, *Literature and Dialectical Materialism*, pp. 16–19.

BIBLIOGRAPHY

Works by D. H. Lawrence

Only works mentioned in the text or notes are listed. The editions given are those cited in the footnotes. Within the brackets the first editions are noted, together with information about rights to the works from which quotations have been made.

Aaron's Rod. New York, Seltzer, 1922. [1st ed., New York, Seltzer, 1922. The American rights of publication are held by the Viking Press, the British by William Heinemann.]

Apocalypse, with an Introduction by Richard Aldington. New York, Viking, 1932. [1st ed., Florence, G. Orioli, 1931. The American rights of publication are held by the Viking Press, the British by William Heinemann.]

Assorted Articles. London, Secker, 1932. [1st ed., London, Secker, 1930. The American rights of publication are held by Alfred A. Knopf, the British by William Heinemann.]

Boy in the Bush, The. New York, Albert & Charles Boni, 1930. [1st ed., London, Secker, 1924. The American rights of publication are held by the Viking Press, the British by William Heinemann.]

Collected Poems. New York, Cape & Smith, 1929. [1st ed., London, Secker, 1928. The American rights

Collected Poems (*Continued*)
of publication are held by the Viking Press, the British by William Heinemann.]

Etruscan Places. New York, Viking, 1933. [1st ed., London, Secker, 1932.]

Fantasia of the Unconscious. London, Secker, 1933. [1st ed., New York, Seltzer, 1922. The American rights of publication are held by the Viking Press, the British by William Heinemann.]

Introduction to Maurice Magnus's Memoirs of the Foreign Legion. [1st ed., London, Secker, 1924.]

Kangaroo. London, Heinemann, 1935. [1st ed., London, Secker, 1923. The American rights of publication are held by the Viking Press, the British by William Heinemann.]

Lady Chatterley's Lover. Florence, privately printed, 1928. [1st ed., Florence, privately printed, 1928. The American rights of publication are held by Alfred A. Knopf.]

Last Poems, edited by Richard Aldington and Giuseppe Orioli, with an Introduction by Richard Aldington. New York, Viking, 1933. [1st ed., Florence, G. Orioli, 1932. The American rights of publication are held by the Viking Press, the British by William Heinemann.]

Letters of D. H. Lawrence, The, edited and with an Introduction by Aldous Huxley. London, Heinemann, 1932. [1st ed., London, Heinemann, 1932. The American rights of publication are held by the Viking Press, the British by William Heinemann.]

Lost Girl, The. New York, Seltzer, 1921. [1st ed., London, Secker, 1920.]

Mornings in Mexico. New York, Knopf, 1934. [1st ed., London, Secker, 1927. The American rights are held by Alfred A. Knopf, the British by William Heinemann.]

Movements in European History. Oxford, Oxford University Press, 1925. [1st ed., London and Oxford, Humphrey Milford, 1921. The British rights are held by the Clarendon Press, Oxford.]

Phoenix, the Posthumous Papers of D. H. Lawrence, edited and with an Introduction by Edward D. McDonald. New York, Viking, 1936. [1st ed., New York, Viking, 1936. The American rights of publication are held by the Viking Press, the British rights by William Heinemann.]

Plumed Serpent, The. London, Secker, 1932. [1st ed., London, Secker, 1926. The American rights of publication are held by Alfred A. Knopf, the British by William Heinemann.]

Psychoanalysis and the Unconscious. London, Secker, 1931. [1st ed., New York, Seltzer, 1921. The American rights of publication are held by the Viking Press, the British by William Heinemann.]

Rainbow, The. [1st ed., London, Methuen, 1915.]

Reflections on the Death of a Porcupine. London, Secker, 1934. [1st ed., Philadelphia, Centaur Press, 1925. The American rights of publication are held by the Centaur Press, the British by William Heinemann.]

Sea and Sardinia. New York, McBride, 1931. [1st ed., New York, Seltzer, 1921. The American rights of publication arc held by the Viking Press, the British by William Heinemann.]

Sons and Lovers. [1st ed., London, Duckworth, 1913.]

Studies in Classic American Literature. New York, Seltzer, 1923. [1st ed., New York, Seltzer, 1923. The American rights of publication are held by the Viking Press, the British by William Heinemann.]

"Studies in Classic American Literature," *The English Review.* Vols. XXVII (November and December, 1918) and XXVIII (January to June, 1919).

Tales of D. H. Lawrence, The. London, Secker, 1934. [1st ed., London, Secker, 1934. This collection contains all of Lawrence's short stories and short novels. The British rights of publication are held by William Heinemann; the American rights to the publication of *St. Mawr*, "Sun," and "Glad Ghosts" are held by Alfred A. Knopf.]

Trespasser, The. [1st ed., London, Duckworth, 1912.]

Twilight in Italy. London, Heinemann, 1934. [1st ed., London, Duckworth, 1916.]

"Unpublished Letters of D. H. Lawrence to Max Mohr, The," *T'ien Hsia Monthly.* Vol. I (August and September, 1935).

White Peacock, The. New York, Duffield, 1911. [1st ed., London, Heinemann, 1911.]

Women in Love. New York, Seltzer, 1922. [1st ed., New York, privately printed, 1920. The American rights of publication are held by the Viking Press, the British by William Heinemann.]

BOOKS AND ESSAYS CONTAINING MATERIAL ABOUT
D. H. LAWRENCE

Arvin, Newton. "D. H. Lawrence and Fascism," *The New Republic,* Vol. LXXXIX (December 16, 1936).

Brett, Dorothy. Lawrence and Brett. Philadelphia, Lippincott, 1933.

Brewster, Earl and Achsah. D. H. Lawrence, Reminiscences and Correspondence. London, Secker, 1934.

Carswell, Catherine. The Savage Pilgrimage. New York, Harcourt, Brace, 1932.

Carter, Frederick. The Dragon of Revelation. London, Harmsworth, 1931.

—— D. H. Lawrence and the Body Mystical. London, Archer, 1932.

Corke, Helen. Lawrence & Apocalypse. London, Heinemann, 1933.

Delavenay, E. "Sur un examplaire de Schopenhauer, annoté par D. H. Lawrence," *Revue Anglo-Américaine,* treizième année (February, 1936).

Douglas, Norman. D. H. Lawrence and Maurice Magnus. Florence, privately printed, 1924.

Eliot, T. S. After Strange Gods. New York, Harcourt, Brace, 1934.

—— Review of J. Middleton Murry's Son of Woman, *The Criterion,* Vol. X (July, 1931).

Fabes, Gilbert H. D. H. Lawrence, His First Editions, Points, and Values. London, Foyle, 1933.

Ford, Ford Madox. Return to Yesterday. New York, Horace Liveright, 1932.

—— "D. H. Lawrence," *The American Mercury,* Vol. XXXVIII (June, 1936).

Gardiner, Rolf. World without End, British Politics and the Younger Generation. London, Cobden-Sanderson, 1932.

Garnett, David. "Reminiscence," in D. H. Lawrence's Love among the Haystacks & Other Pieces. New York, Viking, 1933.

Gregory, Horace. Pilgrim of the Apocalypse. New York, Viking, 1933.

Hone, Joseph. The Life of George Moore. New York, Macmillan, 1936.

James, Henry. Notes on Novelists. New York, Scribner's, 1914.

Kingsmill, Hugh. The Life of D. H. Lawrence. New York, Dodge Publishing Co., 1938.

Lawrence, Ada, and G. Stuart Gelder. Early Life of D. H. Lawrence. London, Secker, 1932.

Lawrence, Frieda. "Not I, but the Wind . . ." New York, Viking, 1934.

Leavis, F. R. D. H. Lawrence. Cambridge, Minority Press, 1930.

Lewis, C. Day. "A Hope for Poetry," in Collected Poems. New York, Random House, 1935.

Lewis, Wyndham. Paleface. London, Chatto and Windus, 1929.

Luhan, Mabel Dodge. Lorenzo in Taos. New York, Knopf, 1932.

McDonald, Edward D. A Bibliography of the Writings of D. H. Lawrence. Philadelphia, Centaur Book Shop, 1925.

—— The Writings of D. H. Lawrence, 1925–1930, a

Bibliographical Supplement. Philadelphia, Centaur Book Shop, 1931.

Merrild, Knud. A Poet and Two Painters. London, Routledge, 1938.

Murry, J. Middleton. Son of Woman. New York, Cape & Smith, 1931.

Phoenix, The, a Quarterly, edited by J. P. Cooney, Woodstock, New York, Vol. I (1938).

Reul, Paul de. L'Œuvre de D.-H. Lawrence. Paris, Vrin, 1937.

Richards, I. A. Science and Poetry. New York, Norton, 1926.

Roberts, John H. "Huxley and Lawrence," *The Virginia Quarterly Review,* XIII (1937), 546–57.

Seillière, Ernest. David-Herbert Lawrence et les récentes idéologies allemandes. Paris, Boivin, 1936.

Spender, Stephen. The Destructive Element. London, Cape, 1935.

Strachey, John. Literature and Dialectical Materialism. New York, Covici, Friede, 1934.

Swerdlow, Irwin. "Lawrence and the Myth," an unpublished Columbia University Master's thesis, 1938.

T., E. D. H. Lawrence, a Personal Record. London, Cape, 1935.

Tindall, W. Y. "D. H. Lawrence and the Primitive," *Sewanee Review,* Vol. XLV (April–June, 1937).

INDEX

Determinism, 49
Diaz, Bernal, 92, 114
Dictatorship, 169, 177
Dionys, Count (character; *see also* Psanek), 102
Doolittle, Hilda (H. D.), 58
Dostoievsky, F. M., 56, 58
Douglas, Norman, 111*n*
Dragon of Revelation, 156, 157
Duality, 65, 66, 67; symbols of, 116

Earth, 76
East, *see* Orient
Easter ceremony, 109
Economic change needed, 163
Economic order, of the past, 183
Education, 46
"Education of the People, The," 66, 101
Edwardian period, 54
Egypt, interest in, 98, 99, 102, 139; symbols of, 140, 143; primitive animism, 143
Einstein, Albert, 31
Eliot, T. S., 183, 190, 192, 198, 200, 203, 206, 209, 210; isolation, 62; Rock, 191 f.; "Dialogue on Dramatic Poetry," 192; *The Waste Land*, 3, 206
Emerson, R. W., 18, 19, 67, 75, 125, 136, 137, 152, 185
Emotions, value of the, 46
England, plan to save from socialism and democracy, 176; Augustan age, 184
English Review, The, 65, 141
Etruscan Places, 86, 119
Etruscans, 99, 118

Fabians, 129, 168
Fairchild, Hoxie Neale, 88; quoted, 193
Fantasia of the Unconscious, 41, 63, 65, 66, 68, 78, 102, 141, 157, 171; Foreword, 71, 150; excerpt, 142
Fascism, 162, 175, 177, 179
Fascist, Lawrence described as, 162, 175, 179

Financiers, *see* Capitalists
Fish, symbolical, 118
Flaubert, Gustave, 32
Flood, Lawrence's prayer for a, 25; pursuit of the antediluvian in tradition of Aztecs, 139; world before the, 145
Flow, 41; the way to reality, 53; in Mrs. Woolf's novels, 55
Flux, *see* Flow
Flying Fish, The, 117
Ford, Ford Madox, 13
"Fox, The," 73
Franklin, Benjamin, 64
Frazer, Sir James G., 101, 111, 143, 144; *Golden Bough*, 97, 155
Freud, Sigmund, 31, 38, 56, 58, 98
Frobenius, Leo, 98, 101, 111, 119, 144, 155, 175*n*

Gamekeepers as heroes, 83, 86, 166
Gardiner, Rolf, 175; *World without End*, 179
Garnett, David, 5
Garnett, Edward, 58
Gaudier-Brzeska, Henri, 89
Gauguin, Paul, 90, 96
George V, literature in reign of, 54
George (character), 70
Gerald (character), 33, 36, 39, 45, 72, 73, 74, 102, 202
Germans, hail Lawrence, 162; in debtedness to, 175; National Socialists, 180
Gipsies, 83
Glacial Period, 142
"Glad Ghosts," 167; excerpt, 38
God, 19, 21
Great Breath, 147, 152
Gregory, Horace, x
Grooms as heroes, 83
Gudrun (character), 34, 40, 47, 72

Haeckel, E. H., 14
Hardy, Thomas, 32, 51, 93, 201, 203
Hargrave, John, *The Confession of the Kibbo Kift*, 176
Harriet (character), 73

A